# UNIVERSE OF THE HUMAN BODY

# UNIVERSE OF THE HUMAN BODY

*with Gaia Touch Body Exercises*

MARKO POGAČNIK

Lindisfarne Books
2016

Lindisfarne Books
an imprint of Anthroposophic Press, Inc.
610 Main Street
Great Barrington, MA 01230
www.steinerbooks.org

ISBN: 978-1-58420-986-7 (print)
ISBN: 978-1-58420-987-4 (ebook)

Printed in the United States of America

# CONTENTS

INTRODUCTION                                                    1

PROLOGUE

Let me introduce Gaia first                                     3
Introducing the idea of the Earthly Cosmos                     4
The phenomenon of the changing Earth                           5
Introducing the idea of an integral anatomy                   7
Introducing Gaia Touch body exercises                          9
Walking the threefold path                                    10
The Dante Alighieri connection                                13


PART 1 — THE HORIZONTAL PATH

1. The Causal World of our Back Space
   and the Daylight World

Front space and back space polarity                           16
Introducing the concept of the causal world                   17
Breaking down the wall                                         18
Our own fear is our greatest enemy                            19
Relating to the body of the planet                            21

2. Gaia's Creative Hand

The composition of Gaia's creative hand                       25
An overview of Gaia's creative hand                           27
Where does the symbolism of the four fingers originate?       28
A short introduction to the elemental world                   29
The personal elemental being                                  30

3. The Plant at the Core of Our Human Identity

Experiencing the plant world   34
The plant at the backbone of the human body   35
The flute of Gaia   38
The feminine aspect of our plant body   40

4. We Share the Miracle of Being Alive with
the Animal Kingdom

Animals are close relatives of the human race   42
The zodiac representing the cosmic status of animals   43
Animals are beyond the zoological dogmas   45
The animal aspect of the human body   46
Animals created conditions for human heart system
to manifest   49

5. The Fairy Ancestors of the Human Race

The elemental civilization of the Earth   51
Our fairy ancestors   53
The elemental self of the human being   55
Sidhe as a parallel to human evolution   56
The subtle fairy body hidden within the human figure   59

6. The Human Being Manifested

The binary rhythm of the human presence in the
Earthly Cosmos   63
The soul as a focus of common human identity   65
The human being on its way toward embodiment   67
The soul's window into infinity   70

7. Can Ego Be Considered as Somebody?

The limitless spectrum of human roles   73
The human being as a being of freedom   74
The human being and the art of life   76

8. The Marvel of Matter

The lithosphere at the base of the world of form   78
A dangerous human intervention   80
Minerals are at the core of human creation   83

INTERMEZZO I

Human beings are leaning heavily upon animals 85
New proportions between extensions of the human being 86
We climb along the vertical world axis 87
The key importance of the Earth's noosphere 89
Take care, dangerous realms! 91
Geocentric or heliocentric? 92


PART II — THE VERTICAL PATH


1. The Gaia-Centered Earthly Cosmos
   A Slovenian Gaia mythos 96
   The Grail mythos addresses the threefold gift of Gaia 98
   The Grail mythos warns us not to abandon our
   relationship with the Earth Soul 101
   Gaia as a potent Creatress 103
   The pattern of Gaia as Mother Earth is out of date 104
   The body of the oceans is Gaia's vehicle of expression 106
   Gaia's oceans and the human water body 107
   Pan as Gaia's masculine complement 109
   The masculine principle as manifested in the human body 111

2. Atomic Power — Dragon Consciousness
   Dragons represent the primeval powers of the Earth 115
   A short history of dragons 116
   Dramatics of the "Atomic Age" 117
   To visit the dragon house in a systematic way 120
   Dragons in effect are angelic beings of the Earth 122
   The dragon resonance within the human body 123
   The role of dragon powers in human creativity 126

3. SOPHIA, THE DIVINE FEMININE
   The patriarchal pattern needs to be transmuted first 128
   The Goddess principle 130
   Sophia's mandorla, the seed of creation 131
   The Goddess of Grace 135
   The Mistress of Dark Powers 137

The sword of truth 139
Christ as the masculine face of Sophia 140
To experience the Christ as a cosmic presence 142

4. ANGELIC MEMBRANES — THE COSMIC CONSCIOUSNESS
Angelic networks are spread throughout the universe 145
Angelic hosts are collaborating with the Earth and its evolution 147
The angelic network within Gaia's lithosphere 148
The role of the lithospheric angels in the human body 150

INTERMEZZO II

Gaia's creative hand — the third continuation 154
The passage through an interdimensional portal 156
The twelve-dimensional blueprint of the Earthly Cosmos 157
A spherical model of the human being 159
The language of dreams 161

PART III — WALKING THROUGH THE HUMAN BODY

1. Visiting the Home of the Personal Elemental Being
Where is the door to enter the body's underground? 164
The personal elemental being is identical to "the body
intelligence" 165
A general blockade of the personal elemental being 167
The elemental being and the integral path of thinking 169
The elemental being holds a permanent link to the
sources of life 171
The personal elemental master 174
Reconnecting with the personal elemental master 175

2. The Architecture of the Body
The present body and the future body 178
The bones as the foundation of the body 180
The skin — the facade of the body 182
The black skin layer 185
The silky grey skin layer 187

3. Materials Composing the House of the Body

The body is primarily a water body 188
Getting rid of the "old luggage" 191
The sacred functions of blood 192
The threat of losing the Thread of Life 193
What about muscles? 196
The role of the fire body 198
Changes concerning body materials 199

4. The Heart System

The superficial projections blocking the heart system 204
The constellation of the heart centers 206
Grounding the heart system 208
The elemental heart 210
Water makes the space of the heart alive 210
The back side of the heart system 212

5. The Creative Scale of the Body Organs

The symmetrical composition of the organs 215
The vortex of polarized organs 215

6. The Mystery of the Head

The all-prevailing presence of the head in the body 220
The body's three-head consciousness 221
The second Chinese Wall 223
The doorway to the brain cavity 225
The frozen treasure of the head 226
The causal dimension of the brain cavity 231
Gaia's creative hand and the human face 233

7. The Multidimensional Body

The human body and the five elements 234
The integral body — the body's future constitution 237

CONCLUSION 239

List of Gaia Touch Exercises 241
List of Drawings 244

# INTRODUCTION

Much knowledge has been gathered during the last three decades about the multidimensional body of the Earth, its landscapes and its different places. To give a name to this kind of experiential science we speak of "geomancy." Geomancy represents an aspect of the Gaia-related culture that has been developing recently on our home planet.

The present work touches upon another facet of Earth's landscape, its smallest unit, which we know as the human body. The human body is as complete in its different dimensions as the landscape, yet it is structured in a different way. The book that you hold in your hand is a sincere attempt to decode the integral human body in the context of what I call the "Earthly Cosmos."

Using my experience of exploring the landscape from my geomantic work, I approach the human body in a similar way, through a kind of multidimensional perception. It means, in this case, to enter one's own body space in a subtle manner and to experience its different extensions from inside. Experiences need to be formulated in a logical way and called by their "proper name." Language has to be invented to express findings in such a way as to become accessible to others who seek to clarify their identity as participants in the evolution of the Earthly Cosmos.

I am lucky to have help in this work from my artist colleague Simona Čudovan. We have worked during the last two years, parallel with each other, on the same themes and aspects of the human presence on Earth. Afterward we shared our experiences, thus correcting and complementing our insights. I wish to express my deep gratitude for her precious collaboration.

Since our mental knowledge cannot be complete without a body-related experience, most of the themes addressed in this book are complemented with exercises. As we are dealing here with the body and its subtle dimensions, all 52 exercises presented in this book include a body exercise. I call them "Gaia Touch body cosmograms." While reading through the book, do not feel obliged to do all the exercises. Rather look at them, and if you feel attracted to some of them, try them, to create a pause during your reading. If you wish to focus upon some subject discussed, return later to the corresponding exercise and integrate it for a certain period into your praxis of daily meditation.

My experience of the last 15 years shows that a succession of subtle changes going on within the human body is supported by the global Earth transformation process. It is not wise to ignore these changes. Doing so may lead to difficulties after the high tide of change has reached the level of day-to-day reality. I believe this work offers an opportunity to better understand what is going on within our bodies and to help us catch up with the transformation process.

*Šempas, October 7, 2014, Marko Pogačnik*

# PROLOGUE

*Let me introduce Gaia first*

There is no doubt: if we continue to ignore Gaia, the source of life and the core consciousness of our home planet, then there will be no way to escape the devastating effects of the so-called "Climate Changes." As a global civilization we are merely moving across the surface of the Earth, not willing to experience the depth and the width of her consciousness.

But who is Gaia beyond the Greek image of the Earth Goddess? Those interested in renewing a loving and caring relationship with our planetary home should pay attention to the Earth's ancient name, hidden in terms like "geology," "geography," "geometry," "geomancy," etc. It is derived from the name of the Greek Goddess of the Earth, Gea or Gaia.

There are two different concepts of our home planet, which need to be clearly distinguished. The modern use of the term "Earth" is related to the image of our planet as a dense ball of matter revolving around the Sun, the star of our planetary system. Yet many of us, feeling a deep kinship with our living planet, are ashamed before such a rather mechanistic image of the Earth, even if it is rationally correct. The rediscovery of our planet as "Gaia" is a welcome alternative, allowing us to imagine the Earth as:

- a living organism
- a sacred place in the universe
- a vast consciousness
- feminine in nature

This vision of Gaia may help to free our awareness from rationalistic images projected upon our beloved planet. Yet, what really counts in life is experience. Could a human being, relatively smaller then an ant, intimately experience this gigantic woman?

Of course, it is possible because Gaia is nothing bigger then our personal identity, since each human being—like each plant, animal, landscape, ocean, etc.—is embodying one of the facets of her living presence. Also, seen from another side, Gaia represents an aspect of our human identity that has been in the process of developing since human beings started to incarnate upon this wonderful planet, penetrating deeper and deeper into interaction with its kingdoms of life.

## Introducing the idea of the Earthly Cosmos

The phrase "Earthly Cosmos" should be understood as complementary to the name of Gaia. While Gaia represents the soul essence of the Earth planet, I call the region of her creation "Gaia's Earthly Cosmos." My intention is to let the artificial division between Cosmos and Earth fall apart. This false division conveys to us that the cosmic dimensions relate to the divine worlds of spirit, while the Earth is the home of matter and other heavy stuff.

This is not true! My experience shows that inherent within the Gaia consciousness is everything that the cosmos is, and vice versa. The cosmos in all its dimensions is present within the worlds of Gaia. In the modern geomancy movement we emphasize the importance of the rule of "holon"—the Greek word for "wholeness." The human body for example is a holon, meaning that everything that exists within the Earthly Cosmos finds a way to express also within the human body. A landscape also represents a complete holon, meaning that places of life power and focuses of consciousness are to be found in every landscape, similar to those that pulsate within the human being, or respectively within the Earthly Cosmos.

Planet Earth is a holon too, which means that all dimensions existing in the universe find their expression within the multidimensional sphere. The same applies to the solar system. And finally, the universe is a holon also, of which Gaia's creation is but a tiny part.

Another concept that needs to be introduced to better get to know Gaia (The Goddess of the Earth holon) is her "noosphere." This word is derived from Greek "noos" meaning "consciousness." Noosphere is complementary to the often-used concept of "biosphere." While biosphere addresses the Earth as a living organism composed of life forces and organic processes, noosphere relates to the Earth as a vast sphere of consciousness. We all are part of Gaia's diverse layers of consciousness: plants, animals, minerals, human beings, landscapes, angelic beings, oceans, elemental beings, etc.

To make it clear, Gaia's manifested body is composed of

- a complex noosphere
- a life sustaining biosphere
- a sphere composed of minute particles of matter that make it possible for some of us, beings of Gaia, to enjoy embodiment in material form

The three spheres of Gaia's body are obviously not separated from each other, but intertwining; they vibrate in a vivid interaction, together creating the wonderful body of the Earthly Cosmos. What today we call "geomancy" is a medial form between art and science, working on research related to the Earthly Cosmos and its diverse dimensions.

## The phenomenon of the changing Earth

As long as the Earth is perceived as a dense ball of matter rotating around the Sun, the changes that ever occur upon the Earth can have only physical causes, like movements of the continental plates, earthquakes, volcanic eruptions, collisions with meteorites, etc. It is not my intention to deny the fatal effects of such events or processes upon the face of the Earth. But the concept of physical Earth Changes has to undergo a radical change if we accept the notion of the Earth as an intelligent being.

Though from the human point of view these are catastrophes and what seem to be chance events, they could be the physical effects of Gaia's conscious intention: the geographical body of the planet and its inhabitants being led through more or less severe changes toward a more perfect and diversified outcome, improving the quality and beauty of our planetary home.

The concept of Gaia' noosphere explains all of the earth's activities. Moving glaciers over large areas of landscapes, the eruptions of volcanoes, great floods, etc. can be understood as specific and goal-orientated interventions of Gaia's creative hand. Gaia has no other tools or machinery at her disposal to work on developing her living and breathing surface organism. Erosion, for example, usually bears a negative connotation, but it becomes just another of Gaia's tools to create the great diversity of landscapes and biotopes upon the Earth's surface.

Yet the situation has changed drastically during the last two centuries. Human beings have developed a civilization on the planet capable of causing unprecedented changes upon the face of the Earth. The development of an astonishing multilayered culture with all its creative achievements is contradicted by ever more absurd building activity, exploitation of Earth's mineral treasures, atomic testing, genetic manipulation of living organisms, and so called "geo-engineering." All this is deeply disturbing to the Earth's atmospheric cycles.

But I firmly believe that people's assumption of "Climate Change" as Gaia's revenge is anthropocentric nonsense, a projection of human psychology upon the wisdom of Gaia's cosmic consciousness. Comparing the present-day Earth Changes with the archetypal pattern of the four elements may sound a clear note that we are not facing a cataclysmic upheaval, but a systemic change of Gaia's planetary body:

- Element Earth: earthquakes and volcano eruptions
- Element Water: unprecedented floods worldwide
- Element Air: winds, typhoons, and whirlwinds of extreme power and speed
- Element Fire: large wild fires that can not be extinguished for weeks at a time

According to my perception, we find ourselves in the midst of a process that has two faces. The destructive one is its superficial aspect—not to understate its violent character, and deeply honoring its victims. It is logical to expect that a world structure, constantly under the stress of egocentric human projections, manipulations of nature, and attempts to control the life processes, must collapse at some point.

More important for our future and the future of our home planet is the positive face of the changes, which I call the "Earth Transmutation Process." As the word "transmutation" suggests, it not only has to do with superficial changes, but also with transformative changes within the subtle layers of the Earth. For almost 17 years I have been closely observing an astonishing succession of changes emanating from the core of the Earth and settling down behind the scenery of the material world. Reports about these rather hidden developments are to be found in my books *Turned Upside Down* and *Gaia's Quantum Leap*.

I believe that Gaia, in cooperation with her cosmic partners, is preparing conditions for a new space-and-time structure of her manifested body to gradually emerge in the present-day epoch. These conditions will allow those extensions of the Earthly Cosmos, nowadays considered non-existent or at least invisible, to become part of the manifested reality in their own way. This does not mean that the material character of our touchable world will be lost. Rather the manifested world will become liberated from human projections that made it become too dense, detaching it from other more sublime dimensions of existence. Parallel with the liberating process, multidimensional portals will start to open again, allowing our consciousness a more open passage between different dimensions of the earthly universe.

Gaia, the Mother of Life, decided to set these double-phase changes into motion—both the positive and destructive phases— to prevent the deterioration of the vital capacities of the Earth. Like all the inhabitants of the Earthly Cosmos, the human race cannot avoid being involved. To be able to continue enjoying the beauty and creative challenges of this wonderful planet, we must continuously adapt to the changes generated by the ongoing Earth transformation process.

Yet understanding the concept is not enough. Changes touch all levels of existence, *not just in the mental sense, but also bodily*. Understanding the multidimensional nature of our own body, and consciously cooperating with the changes involved, can help us as embodied beings to follow the winding path of the present Earth Changes.

### Introducing the idea of an integral anatomy

As a human being, I am one of the beings of Gaia with the luck to be embodied in a relatively dense form of minute particles of matter. As a sculptor, I wish I had been born in the epoch of the High

Renaissance when the material body of the human being was discovered anew. What a powerful stream of inspiration was drawn upon by the artists of that epoch, such as Leonardo da Vinci and Michelangelo Buonarroti, who secretly cut up human cadavers in order to unveil the structure under the skin! Trespassing a severe taboo, they were committing a crime according to the rules set by the medieval Christian Church. That stream of inspiration has vanished, but the anatomy of the human body has been laid bare to the last nerve during the last two centuries.

Up until the present, anatomy has brought us knowledge mostly of the physical human body. The third millennium brings a new focus to both the subconscious and the submaterial bodies within Gaia and all of her manifested beings, humans included: to study the manifested results of the Earth transmutation process that I mentioned. The purpose of this book, and much of my recent work, is to enlarge the knowledge and the experience of what may be called the "integral anatomy" of the human body, reflected in the mirror of the Earthly Cosmos.

What do I mean by the concept of integral anatomy? The word "anatomy" comes from the Greek verb "anatemnein," which means "cutting into pieces." The word is in our case used to focus on the separate aspects of our multidimensional body, to look at them in the context of their geomantic background. "Geomantic" means perceived in the context of the multidimensional Earth body.

To be clear, we are not dealing with classical anatomy, but with an integral approach. With this approach to anatomy, we are not going to separate the human being into pieces. In the first step we need to focus our interest on the separate aspects and dimensions of the human body—to take them out of the old narrow concepts of the material body, experience them in their essence, and integrate them into the all-connecting cosmos of the human body.

There should be no confusion about my liberal use of the term "body." As in the case of the Earth body, usually identified with the material shell of Gaia, the human body is, in our rationally orientated culture, considered primarily as an object composed of organic matter. By detaching it from this limiting concept, I wish to present the human body as a multi-storied house with many rooms. It is the house in which the human being abides while evolving and creating within the Earthly Cosmos—whether incarnated or not. My intention is to lead you through the different rooms of your own house, making you aware of the treasures that are stored there at different levels. All these treasures are potentials of your being to be activated and used in this present moment of change, making you capable of meeting its challenges.

### Introducing Gaia Touch body exercises

To insure the practical value of this book and to be of help in the process of personal changing, the text is as short as possible, giving enough space for individual experience through the exercises. The Gaia Touch exercises are offered throughout the whole book as an invitation to gather your own experiences on the themes discussed. The exercises can be done parallel to reading the book. It is also possible just to look through them and decide later which ones to practice over a certain period of time.

Gaia Touch body exercises are primarily dedicated to deepening the relationship between human beings and the Earthly Cosmos. They were inspired by elementary and other beings of many sacred places of the Earth. Beings of Gaia consciousness have offered them to human beings to help us attune better to the multidimensional nature of our home planet and to the other inhabitants who belong to different levels of reality. The exercises represent a combination of body movements and imaginations, a kind of yoga dedicated to cooperation with Gaia and her noosphere.

I started to perceive and formulate the Gaia Touch exercises one by one after the year 1998 when the above-mentioned Earth transmutation process arrived at the threshold of my awareness. Seen in the context of the Earth Changes, the purpose of the Gaia Touch exercises is to stimulate personal development in such a way that the practitioner will be able to attune to the new emerging reality and to prepare the different body dimensions for the coming changes—even more, to be able to embody them when they knock on one's door.

Gaia Touch exercises are a specific form of cosmograms. Cosmograms represent an aspect of the universal language. I started to use the term "cosmogram" to address language forms that can be perceived not just by human beings, but also by other beings of the Earth and the universe. Cosmograms find their expression both on the material level and on the invisible etheric level, which can be perceived by beings that have no capacity to see physical forms. Vice versa, as a language based upon the laws of sacred geometry, geomancy, archetypal forms, etc., cosmograms are capable of transporting multilayer messages.

The authentic power of the Gaia Touch body cosmograms is generated by the consciousness and beings of those sacred places that inspired them. The beings are usually mentioned in the commentaries of each exercise. The exercises also work in a complementary direction. By performing a Gaia Touch exercise one supports the given place and its beings in their striving to reveal the true identity of their place and to strengthen its unique contribution to the life processes upon the Earth.

It is important to know that Gaia Touch exercises work through the interaction between the body movements and the capacity of imagination. It is not necessary to have in mind the background of an exercise while performing it; but it is necessary to know the purpose of the exercise, and which of its movements needs to be supported by your imagination. Enter the world of the exercise without projections, and allow yourself to be carried by its wings.

The exercise I offer to experience the Gaia Touch method comes from Crete, a large island in the Mediterranean. It was inspired by Minoan clay figurines, made over three millennia ago, of a Goddess with raised arms. While working there in the framework of a geomantic workshop, together with my daughter Ana, we came in contact with the ancient Minoan culture, a Goddess-centered culture, which obviously stood in a vital relationship with the creative forces of Gaia. This can be perceived through the traces of their joyful close-to-nature art works, depicted on the frescoes found in the ruins of the Minoan palaces.

*Walking the threefold path*

Dear co-traveler, to make our future path through the dimensions of the integral human body secure, we need to obtain a proper key

CRETE EXERCISE TO STRENGTHEN THE RELATIONSHIP
WITH GAIA

1. Stand upright, and focus on the center of your body.

2. Sink to the earth by bending your knees, as much as you can without losing your balance. This symbolizes: the universe getting closer to the Earth.

3. Holding this position, lift your arms, half-angled, until your palms reached the height of your throat. Your elbows stick out a little bit on each side. This symbolizes: the Earth getting closer to the universe.

4. Stay for a while in this position—as long as you can. Be attentive to feelings that may arise within you.

5. Stand up again, and draw a large circle around you with your outstretched hands, starting at the lowest point that you can easily reach and ending above your head. The circle represents: the whole spectrum of different worlds that Gaia is upholding and nourishing inside her "Earthly Cosmos"—the vast space between the universe and the Earth.

6. It is advisable to repeat the exercise a few times and then observe what is going on within you.

that can open a door leading to the different extensions of the integral human body. My intuition offers a key in the form of the "cosmic cross." The arms of the cosmic cross are equally long, perfectly centered, and the space they encompass is rounded up by a circle representing the universal whole. This symbol has been known to human cultures since the Paleolithic era.

The cosmic cross, as a symbol of the cosmic whole, has a spherical variation with the addition of a third axis at a right angle to the intersection of the arms of the cross. I will call it "the spherical axis." Our journey through the Earthly Cosmos and the universe of the human body will lead us through the three arms of the spherical cross. Let me give a brief outline of the planned journey:

Walking *the horizontal arm of the cosmic cross* we will pass through the spectrum of life processes evolving upon the Earth, meeting different beings, visible and invisible, who inhabit the planet. What we are interested in are the resonances of all these beings and dimensions upon the human body. The path has two parts, corresponding to the back and front sides of our body. The back side refers to the causal world, working from behind the scenery of everyday life. The front side has to do with all the different aspects of life manifested in the material world.

*The vertical arm of the cosmic cross* stands for the spectrum of beings and powers extending between the center of the Earth and the core of the universe, traditionally called the "axis of the world." We will begin our journey from the lowest point of the axis, the divine home of Gaia, passing through the region of their archetypal powers, called "dragons," to reach its highest point, home of Gaia's cosmic counterpart, Sophia. We shall observe how different worlds and dimensions of the Earthly Cosmos reflect within the human body.

The third path will lead us through *the center of the cosmic cross.* In effect we will be walking along the third, the spherical, axis of the cross archetype. The path will lead us through the inner worlds of the body, through its organic architecture, through the different organs, layers of the skin, etc. We will visit the home of the individual's elemental being and rejoice at the beauty of the human belly, heart, and head systems.

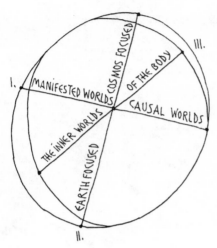

*The threefold path*

## The Dante Alighieri connection

My original inspiration while preparing this book was to update Dante's *Divine Comedy*, written between the 13th and 14th centuries. I recognized that the pattern of the threefold path through the universe of our existence in Dante's epos is related to the traditional shamanic world image of the underworld, the middle world, and the upper world. Dante, in effect, uses the same path through the three world levels, translating them into Christian terminology as Hell, Purgatory, and Paradise.

I am sure that the time is ripe to trace the threefold path in another way, different from both the shamanic perspective and Dante's enlightened Christianity. New times demand that a new matrix be created. So here is my proposal to update the archetype of the threefold world image.

I do not want to anticipate its characteristics. They should speak for themselves. But it may be of help to understand why in the prologue to several chapters I address you, dear reader, personally. It is because in Dante's precious work, he was led through the three world dimensions by Beatrice and the Roman poet Virgil. In the case of the Universe of the Human Body, I myself take over the task to lead you—not through a distant universe, but through the universe of your own being. I hope you will enjoy the journey.

# PART 1
# THE HORIZONTAL PATH

# 1

# THE CAUSAL WORLD OF OUR BACK SPACE AND THE DAYLIGHT WORLD

Before we start our journey I would ask you dear co-traveler to be patient for a moment. I need to clarify several issues that are of crucial importance, so that our path along the horizontal axis of our existence can be understood properly.

*Front space and back space polarity*

The superficial human viewpoint tries to convince us that the daylight world, dancing its often crazy dance in front of our body, represents the whole of reality. It makes us forget that there exists its other half positioned behind our back. Like day and night, both halves complement each other. In other words, the world of the daily events in front of us, illuminated by the bright light of the reasoning mind, is the world of effects only, while the region of their causes is situated in the back space of our body, beyond the control of our eyes.

Since the highly advanced technological culture we live in does not recognize the dark side of reality pulsating behind our backs, we are forced to live permanently under the flash of the daylight control. Not knowing the source of upcoming events, we can only guess their meaning and where they are leading us. Their causes are hidden in the unknown "dark universe" pulsating behind our back.

I am using the wording "dark universe," aware of the scientific theory supposing that 70% of our universe consists of "dark energy"— which could be the unknown cause behind the visible phenomena of the known reality.

I can propose a Gaia Touch exercise to introduce you to the difference between the daylight space in front of the body and the space extending behind its back side. The exercise is based upon different positioning of the feet.

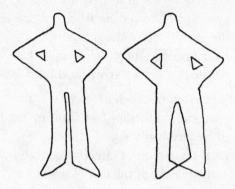

FOOT EXERCISE TO DISTINGUISH THE QUALITIES OF THE FRONT AND THE BACK SPACES

1. While standing, place your feet in the usual manner with heels touching each other and the toes wide apart. In this way you are open toward the manifested world in front of you.

2. Then change the position so that the big toes are touching each other but the heels are spread as widely apart as possible. In this way your back space opens. Listen to its quality.

3. After a while change the position of the feet again. Repeat the exercise a few times, observing the difference between the two sides of the body space.

4. The exercise may also be used as a perception exercise if you turn your back toward a tree or a chosen place and change the position of your feet.

## Introducing the concept of the causal world

To give proper names to both polarities experienced through the above exercise, we usually speak of the *manifested* world in front of the body and the *causal* realm behind the back. This is a symbolic language. If you turn around, it is easy to see that the manifested world is all around you. The same applies to the causal dimension, often labeled "invisible." The following may clarify the different functions of the causal and manifested worlds.

Some characteristics of the causal world:

- It is symbolically positioned behind our back, which means, out of the reach of our five physical senses.

- It represents the region of matrix, where archetypal (primeval) patterns of all phenomena are stored that represent the base of the manifested world.
- It is the liquid aspect of the universe where worlds and beings pulsate that do not know fixed form of existence.

Some characteristics of the manifested world:

- It is symbolically positioned in front of the body to be perceived by physical senses
- It represents the region of effects produced by the causes rooted in the matrix of the causal world.
- It is the solid world of material forms and embodied phenomena of life.

*Breaking down the wall*

Before we proceed towards experiencing the dynamics between the back and the front sides of the body we will need to deal with what could be called "a second Berlin Wall." Why Berlin Wall? Breaking down the wall that once separated the communist East from the capitalist West became a symbol of freedom for the human race. Soon it turned out that tearing down the physical wall did not automatically bring more freedom. Almost thirty years later we are controlled in a more sublime manner then ever before.

The reason for the failure might be the "invisible Berlin Wall," which has not yet been deprived of its separating function. It prevents human beings from freely pass between the fragile scenery of life evolving in front of our body and the causal world behind our back, rooted in the ocean of infinity. Because the wall is separating us individually—and our culture as a whole also—from the sources of Gaia's inspiration and her limitless flow of abundance, the scenery of everyday life becomes extremely fragile. It tends repeatedly to break apart in conflicts, or even wars, and to drown in crises and conditions of scarcity or overloaded wealth.

The wall separating us from the sources of life has to disappear if we as human beings want truly to become beings of freedom. It is not just a matter of changing awareness, what needs to be done

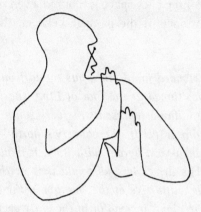

HAND COSMOGRAM TO DISSOLVE THE WALL SEPARATING THE FRONT
FROM THE BACK SIDES OF THE BODY:

1. Position both hands in front of your chest, holding the edges of
   the hands in such a way that the inner side of one hand points
   to the left and its back to the right—the other hand vice versa.
2. Start with circling the edge of one hand around the edge of the
   other hand, while they are continuously touching each other.
   Like two millstones, they are circling around each other.
3. After a while, reverse the direction of the circling.
4. To strengthen the exercise, you can imagine taking the circling "millstones" into your heart space and continue "milling" there.
5. It is not advisable to perform the "milling" exercise too long.
   Rather, take pauses of stillness and feel what the exercise
   has induced within you.

then is the transmutation of a deeply incarnated energetic bound-
ary that runs along the edges of our body. To work on its decomposition I can propose a Gaia Touch exercise. It was given to me
by high elemental beings of a sacred table mountain called Meis-
sner situated, near Kassel in Germany. It is a hand cosmogram.

## Our own fear is our greatest enemy

A recent dream of mine pinpoints a second reason why the free
passage between the daylight world in front of the body and the

liquid universe of the back space is blocked, even when we understand the importance of the passage between the two faces of reality.

*I sit with my extended family in a bus to start our travel to Catania, a town positioned at the foot of Etna, the famous volcano of Sicily. While Catania represents the very south of Italy, we are about to start our travel in the country's north—I live with my family at the north-west border with Italy. It is about a ten-hour bus ride. The bus driver lets us know that at the start we are already late. We will arrive at the "bottom of the Italian boot" in the middle of the night, instead of in the early evening.*

Here it needs to be pointed out that the form of the Apennine peninsula, where Italy is located, is traditionally compared with the human foot, booted in a high heel boot. Sicily then, compared to the human body, would be positioned below our feet. Further translated into the language of logic this would mean that the family sitting in the bus represents a human family on the way to reconnect with somebody situated "below our feet," i.e., with Gaia, the Earth Soul. This notion is underlined by the fact that Catania lies at the foot of the only active volcano in Europe (which has even erupted recently). Consequently, the way to Catania represents the path toward reconnecting with the primeval powers of life emanating from the depth of the Earth.

*Next, the dream lets me know why we are delayed in starting our travel. I am shown a thick grey snake moving along the edge of the body of each of us. It moves slowly, exactly along where the "second Berlin Wall" is situated.*

Translating from the symbolic dream language, this means that without trespassing the border between the daylight world in front and the causal world at the back, the individual process of reconnection with Gaia cannot move forward.

*Next, I am shown the reason that we cannot simply ignore the border division and get on our way. I see that the snake gliding along the edge of the body of one of the travelers makes a little turn around, removing itself for an instant from his body. At that moment I feel enormous fear shaking my whole body, realizing at the same time that this is not just my own individual panic, but a collective fear deeply rooted in the psyche of modern human beings.*

It was not a natural kind of fear, deriving from our animal memory. Animals are not in this kind of fear as they constantly observe their environment for safety. I felt that the pattern of this kind of deeply embedded fear was purposely injected into the human psyche to keep us individually and collectively blocked in our potential capacity to move freely back and forth between the worlds. Now the time has come to get the grey particles of fear out of our body. This dream inspired me to create a Gaia Touch exercise dedicated to this purpose.

The exercise (given on the following page) is meant to be performed standing. See that you have enough space at your back and front to be able to move three steps backward and three steps forward.

### Relating to the body of the planet

Does the Earth's planetary body show a front/back polarity? The answer is not as easy as in the case of the human body, which is not arranged in the same way as Gaia's body. A sphere does not have simply a front side and a back side. By turning it all around, one realizes that each face of a globe is equal in status to all the others. But there must be a way for the body of the Earth to show its front/back polarity: the binary relationship between the daylight (manifested) world and the liquid universe of the causal world!

What about the polarity between mountains and oceans?

The greatest depth of the oceans is in the Pacific Ocean, north of New Zealand; it is comparable to the highest mountains in the Himalayas. If it were possible for the oceans to rise upward into the air like the mountains, then the oceans and seas of the Earth would appear as mountains of water. And what gigantic glittering mountains they would be! In effect, they are mountains

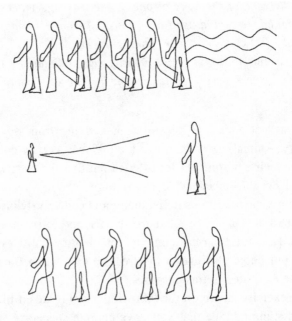

EXERCISE TO RINSE PARTICLES OF FEAR OUT OF THE BODY

1. Imagine that your back space is filled with pure ocean water (representing the liquid universe of the causal world.)

2. Step backward with your left foot, leaning into the pure water of the ocean behind your back and allow its drops to glide through your body, filtering out and transmuting the particles of fear caught like grey dust in your intercellular spaces.

3. Take another step backward with your left foot, followed by another one, always starting with your left foot. Pause between each step to allow the water to glide very slowly through the tissues of your body, drawing out and transmuting the old stock of fear. You can help the process by holding the process in the aura of the color violet, the color of transmutation.

4. Now the minute empty spaces, previously occupied with particles of fear, need to be filled with the positive energy of trust.

5. For this purpose take three steps forward, stepping each time first with your right foot. Imagine that in front of you is the model of the perfect human being that each of us is evolving toward. With each step you are closer to it. Pause between each step to absorb the inspiration deeply into your body.

6. Then, start from the beginning, again going three steps backward, starting with the left foot.

of water that are balancing the mineral mountains of the Earth's continents.

The "mountains of salty water" concentrate and preserve the information of life, thus representing the causal dimension of the Earth's body—later we shall talk in detail about their function. The solid mountain chains represent their complementary pole. The balance between the mountains of water and the solid mountains can be compared with the relationship between the two facets of our body and their corresponding consciousnesses.

Their balance, important for the health of the planet, can be experienced and supported through the following Gaia Touch exercise. It was inspired by the highest mountain (2,864 meters) in the Julian Alps, located in the northwest corner of my home country, Slovenia. The mountain's name is Triglav, which means "The Three-headed One." It is good to know that Triglav is considered to embody the archetype of Slovenia.

While leading a workshop at the foot of the northern wall of Triglav Mountain, at one point I heard a strong voice resounding within me with the words, "I am Himalayas." At first, this sounded strange to me. But in the next moment, I realized that there is a message underlying these words of Triglav affirming that there exists a planetary network interconnecting the great mountain ranges and the individual holy mountains.

The exercise (given on the following page) underscores the balance between the physically interconnected "watery mountains" of seas and oceans and the network of solid mountains. It can be done in groups, or adapted to be done individually.

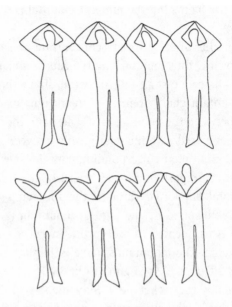

EXERCISE TO GIVE THANKS TO THE PLANETARY NETWORK OF
MOUNTAINS AND OCEANS

1. The group stands in a circle.
2. Lift your arms above your head to create a pyramidal form.
   The middle fingers touch each other to form a triangle sym-
   bolizing the peak of the mountain.
3. To recreate the network of mountains, the elbows of the participants should touch. Stay for a while in this position to
   connect to the power of the mountains.
4. Move your hands downward slowly, (without losing the elbow
   connection to your partners, also keeping the middle fingers
   connected) to recreate the depth of the oceans, lakes, and rivers.
5. Stay for a while in this position to experience the soft power
   of our planet's waters.
6. Then, together, start lifting your hands again to embody the
   network of mountains.
7. Repeat the sequence a few times. Then join hands and make a
   deep bow to give thanks for the gifts that we receive constantly
   from the water crystals and the crystals of the mountains.

# 2
# GAIA'S CREATIVE HAND

Moving through the last chapter, we became aware that behind our back exists the liquid universe of the so-called causal dimension. We examined the relationship of the causal dimension to the daylight world in front of our body. The binary rhythm of causes and their effects between these two dimensions is important to understanding the composition of the Earthly Cosmos. We shall use this relationship often during our travels through the extensions of the integral human body. This is the relationship mirroring the horizontal axis of the threefold cosmic cross, reaching from the causal dimension to the material world.

At this point, I wish to touch briefly upon the principle of a "key" and its function in the process of approaching different realms of the Earthly Cosmos. A key/symbol represents one of the basic tools of geomantic research. Holding a key in one's hand indicates that you, as a visitor, having arrived at a gate, are attuned to the essence of a place. As a consequence, deeper layers of the place are ready to open in front of the exploring visitor. In this chapter I wish to present another key that can help orient us on our path through the universe of the Earth and of the human body. I will call it "Gaia's creative hand."

*The composition of Gaia's creative hand*

First let us look upon our own hand. Through our hand, Gaia has bestowed on us the best key for understanding her creation in all its diversity. It is also possible that the human being has been given this extraordinary key so that we become aware of our particular role in the Earthly Cosmos.

Like our own hand, the creative hand of Gaia is composed of a palm and five fingers. To use one's hand as a key, its versatility should first be recognized. Our hand is useful only because the thumb is clearly different in its function from the other four fingers. It is obvious that the four fingers are not capable of doing anything useful if not in cooperation with the thumb. It is also the synergy between four fingers and a thumb that makes Gaia's hand such a wonderfully creative tool.

The four fingers of Gaia's creative hand are the elements of water, fire, earth, and air. The fingers also represent the manifested worlds of plants, animals, minerals, and human beings. Looking upon our hand, we can see that each finger is composed of three knuckles. This indicates that each element appears in the manifested world in a threefold way.

Gaia's forefinger represents the water element:

- The first knuckle is embodied worldwide in the form of oceans, rivers, lakes, etc.
- The second knuckle represents the world of plants.
- The third knuckle represents the biosphere of the Earth.

Gaia's middle finger represents the fire element:

- The first knuckle represents the fire of the Sun, the light during the day and reflected light from the Moon during the night.
- The second knuckle represents the animal kingdom.
- The third knuckle represents the creative processes.

Gaia's ring finger represents the earth element:

- The first knuckle represents the soil.
- The second knuckle is manifested through the mineral world.
- The third knuckle symbolizes processes of embodiment.

Gaia's little finger represents the air element:

- The first knuckle stands for the atmosphere of the planet.
- The second knuckle represents the human being as a being of the Earth.
- The third knuckle symbolizes the element of air as the consciousness sphere (noosphere) of the planet.

The thumb of Gaia's creative hand, the "fifth element," embodies the primeval powers and consciousness of Gaia, including her elemental beings, who operate behind the scene of the manifested world. The fifth element is present all around us. Even when the powers and beings of the causal world do not show a physical body, they are playing a decisive role in how the manifested world comes into existence.

Gaia's thumb, the fifth element, can be represented as follows:

- The first knuckle stands for the world of the elemental beings.
- The second knuckle of the thumb symbolizes the causal world present at the back of embodied reality.
- The third knuckle reveals Gaia's creative hand as the guardian of identity for all beings of the Earth.

The slightly hollow space of the palm, by its central position, stands for the archetypal dimensions of the earthly universe, with their source at the core of the planet. These archetypal dimensions can be identified as the matrix of the Earthly Cosmos, representing the source of the causal level that underlies the manifested world.

The triangle in the palm of Gaia's hand symbolizes Gaia at the core of the Earthly Cosmos:

- Gaia embodies the all-integrating Mother of Life.
- Gaia embodies the divine dimension of the Earth.
- Gaia embodies the archetypal matrix of life.

I wish to also mention that each of the four fingers of Gaia's creative hand has a fourth knuckle, which is hidden. It represents the consciousness dimension of the four elements, and will be discussed later in the section called "Intermezzo I."

## An overview of Gaia's creative hand

Water element (Gaia's forefinger)
    Water worldwide
    World of plants
    Biosphere of the Earth

Fire element (Gaia's middle finger)
    Daylight and night's light
    Animal kingdom
    Life processes

Earth element (Gaia's ring finger)
    The soil
    Mineral world
    Processes of embodiment

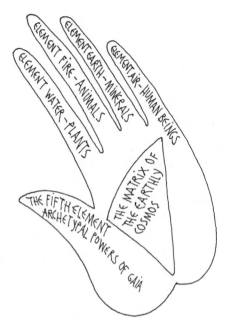

*Gaia's creative hand*

Air element (Gaia's little finger)
   Atmosphere
   Human being as a being of the Earth
   Sphere of consciousness—the noosphere

Fifth element (Gaia's thumb)
   World of the elemental beings
   Causal dimensions of the Earth
   Guardian of identity of all beings of the Earth

Gaia matrix (the palm of Gaia's hand)
   Integrating Mother of life
   Divine dimension of the Earth
   Archetypal matrix of life

## *Where does the symbolism of the four fingers originate?*

It is possible that this imagery of the four fingers in relationship
to the four elements differs from the usual attributions. The given
symbolism relates to the four circles of the four-element chakras

of the human body that years ago I discovered and identified together with my daughter Ajra. The system is published in my book *Sacred Geography*. This discovery is the result of our search to balance the masculine character of the well-known vertical system of seven chakras with a feminine-quality chakra system.

The four-element chakras are positioned in a circular way around the heart chakra (the heart chakra representing the "Fifth Element") Standing upright, with feet and hands apart (outstretched), it is easy to imagine the four chakra circles of the body as follows:

- The first circle stands for the water element, with resonance at the forefinger. Its chakras are positioned above the chest and below both clavicles, with the next pair above the kidneys.

- The second circle represents the fire element, with resonance at the middle finger. Its chakras can be found at the ear lobes, at the shoulders, and at the hips.

- The third circle stands for the earth element, with resonance at the ring finger. Its chakras pulsate behind the elbows, behind the knees, and at the end of the imagined "tail."

- The fourth circle symbolizes the air element, with resonance at the small finger. Its chakras can be found in the palms of the hands and the soles of the feet, as well as one above the head.

## A short introduction to the elemental world

The themes related to Gaia's creative hand will be examined in detail in a discussion of the extensions of the integral human body. First, I wish to present briefly the essence of my knowledge of the world of elemental beings, collected through my geomantic work of the last 25 years. This summary is meant for readers who are not familiar with the wonderful world of the elemental beings.

The elemental beings uphold an extremely important bridge, the purpose of which is the translating of Gaia's ideas and impulses into forms and constellations in the manifested everyday world.

They perform their services through invisible causal extensions of the Earthly Cosmos. They are the transition of Gaia's creative process between the archetypal blueprints of Gaia's matrix and the formation of shining landscapes, living beings, and other phenomena on the Earth's surface. There would be no daily life manifested in the material world without the joyful activity of the multitude of these diverse elemental beings.

The world of elemental beings is structured according to the pattern of the four elements, i.e., according to the four fingers of Gaia's creative hand:

> *Water element:* elemental beings embodying the noosphere of lakes, rivers, and other smaller water bodies; beings of the oceans; masters of emotional qualities.

> *Fire element:* elemental beings embodying processes of change, decay, and regeneration; beings of cosmic wisdom; carriers of artistic inspiration.

> *Earth element:* elemental beings guiding formative processes in the landscape; guiding the growth of plants, animals, humans, and crystals, and creating etheric molds for all existing forms so that they can appear (in collaboration with the minerals) as manifested phenomena.

> *Air element:* elemental beings monitoring the cycles of nature, attuning them to cosmic cycles; coloring the atmosphere of places with qualities; supervising the cycles of evolution and individual destiny of manifested beings.

## The personal elemental being

The position of the human being in relation to the elemental kingdom is not much different from that of plants, animals, or landscapes. Incarnated upon the Earth, the human being needs to be cared for in a similar way as a plant or an animal. Now, I would like to bring to awareness and make clear that a human being should be considered as a being of the Earth, and that like a plant, an animal, and a mineral, also has an associated elemental being. The personal elemental being of a human individual has much to do:

*Beings of the earth element (dwarves) work on transforming archetypes into living forms. A cosmogram created for a children's book.*

- All the different aspects and organs of our body, in every moment, have to be attuned to each other properly so that we can be fit and healthy. All the causal and material dimensions of our being, in every moment, must be attuned as a whole to its matrix.
- Our thinking processes have to be plugged into the corresponding memory capacities of the Earth's noosphere.
- Energy conditions and life situations have to be placed onto our life path at the right moment, so that we can learn and create in an optimal way.
- During the process of human incarnation care must be taken for the balanced evolution of the developing fetus. After its departure from the manifested world all the layers of the individual's body must be cleaned and returned to Gaia because they belong to Gaia's noosphere.

As in the case of a plant, the human being is asked to share "its house"—the body—with an elemental being in a lifelong commitment. "The house" we share with our elemental being is identical with our personal holon. The elemental being abides and moves within our water body. Because the emotional consciousness of our water body encompasses our holon completely, our personal elemental can freely penetrate all extensions of our manifested body, navigating within its noosphere. In this way it can reach all the organs and energy centers of the body's organism to work on their attunement and equilibration.

These are ideal conditions, of course. Unfortunately we humans create many obstacles to the personal elemental being, instead of supporting its wonderful service to our life. By our holding stubbornly onto traumas and blockades that cause parts of our emotional sphere to freeze, the personal elemental is prevented from approaching the corresponding organs. Then the organs cannot be kept in perfect balance, and health problems may arise.

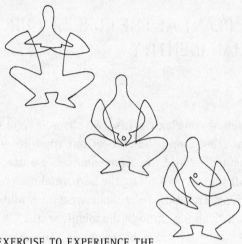

### GAIA TOUCH EXERCISE TO EXPERIENCE THE PERSONAL ELEMENTAL BEING

1. Sit down in peace for a while and ask in silence your personal elemental being to show itself to you so that mutual links of love and cooperation can be reestablished.

2. With palms upward, position your hands horizontally in front of your heart and connect with the imagination of a water field, or perhaps a large shallow pond, inside your heart space. The personal water sphere image should reach a bit beyond the boundaries of your body.

3. Lower your hands to the level of the solar plexus, which represents the central region of your water body and is one of the focal points of your personal elemental being.

4. Imagine holding a little pebble in front of your solar plexus in one of your hands.

5. Throw the pebble upward with the help of the corresponding hand gesture, so that it falls into the pond. The gesture must be carried out energetically, so that the elemental being can perceive it.

6. Do not hesitate. In the moment the pebble has fallen into the pond, start to observe the reaction of the water surface as the pebble falls toward the bottom of the pond—listen to the echo of your action. If needed, repeat the exercise a few times.

# 3

# THE PLANT AT THE CORE OF OUR HUMAN IDENTITY

Dear fellow traveler, the first two chapters were needed to prepare for traveling along the path of our tripartite journey in mutual understanding and free from some basic obstacles. At this point, we will start to walk along the horizontal path of the cosmic cross archetype. Traditional shamanic wisdom would call our horizontal path "walking through the middle world."

We will first move backward in the direction of the causal world (behind our back). The first dimension to visit is the plant world. We shall approach it with the question in mind: "Is there an aspect of the human being related to the delicate world of plants?" Humans look so different from plants. Are plants in some way our relatives?

*Experiencing the plant world*

Before we can answer this question, we need some insights into the marvelous world of plants and their purpose within the multidimensional organism of the planet.

Plants are primeval daughters of Gaia. Looking at a plant, I can feel within my body the power that grows directly from the core of the planet. It is the same immense inner power that a sprout embodies as it strives to break through the Earth's crust to appear in the realm of daylight.

Plants represent a large collective spread over the Earth. It is the plant collective that has the task of upholding and constantly renewing the paradise-like quality of places and landscapes. As the oldest settlers upon the Earth's surface, they are entitled to transmit the serenity, beauty, and peace of Gaia to the worlds and beings that populate the landscapes and continents. Looking with our inner eyes it is possible to see the peace and love impulses distributed throughout the landscape via the plant world. Like the birds and insects joyously flying, sounding the song of life, plants deliver the message of Gaia in a silent but no less powerful way—as much as the machinery of modern civilization still allows it to manifest, of course.

Plants, as large organisms such as forests, perform through their silent activity another important service in life. They create holon-like spherical spaces, which are distributed all over the face of the Earth. I perceive these as subtle "houses" made of fine membranes. These subtle spaces become inhabited, developed further, and used by other beings, constituting the vital, living organism of the landscape. Without these delicate holon-like divisions the Earth's surface would be an utter void, foreign to any living or cultural development.

Interestingly, attuning to a plant, I perceive a silent activity similar to that within my own body. Delicate micro-spheres appear inside my body, similar to air bubbles. Yet their nature is not airy, but rather of watery quality. I perceive these same watery bubbles within a plant's body as a tool to heighten its sensitivity. Here the link of the plant world to the element of water comes into expression. The presence of water in my body enables the subtle extensions of my being to find a place to pulsate within my physical organism. Am I as a human being also taking part in the subtle life of plants?

I can propose a Gaia Touch exercise (given on the following page) to gather more experiences concerning the wonderful beings of plants.

## The plant at the backbone of the human body

I first experience our connection with the plant world as hidden in the human capacity to stand upright, connected to the core of the Earth. This affirms our identity as beings of Gaia.

My intention is not to question the importance of the backbone; our capacity to stand upright and to move around is a brilliant creation of Gaia's architecture. I believe the backbone is the physical manifestation of our "plant stem." Behind the upright posture of the human being lies the strength of the stalk of grain, shooting vertically out of the Earth, as if coming directly from the

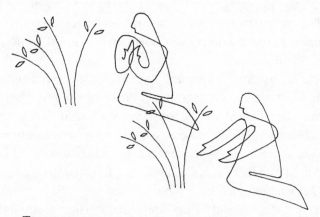

GAIA TOUCH EXERCISE TO PERCEIVE THE ESSENCE OF PLANTS

1. Standing in front of a chosen plant, communicate that you are approaching it from the level of your heart. To address a small plant, come close to it by sitting or kneeling in front of it.

2. Show to the plant your intent through the following gesture: Point your hands toward your heart to pinpoint the level you intend to use to enter into communion with the plant.

3. Immediately afterward, with a movement in the opposite direction, turn your hands toward the plant with an opening gesture.

4. With the gesture that moves again toward your heart, imagine that you are taking the essence of the plant close to your heart.

5. Repeat this back and forth movement a few times, so that the plant can notice it. Be present in a loving way.

6. Become still and listen to the plant. If needed, repeat the gestures after a while.

core of Gaia, to stand erect even in the face of a whirling wind.

This plant-like dimension of the human body can be imagined as a light tube standing vertically through the middle of our body space. It has its source at the core of the Earth—in the "heart of Gaia"—running upward through our body to connect with the core of the Sun, Earth's home star.

One can imagine the Earth and the Sun as parents of the plant world. The life of a plant oscillates between the fecundity of the

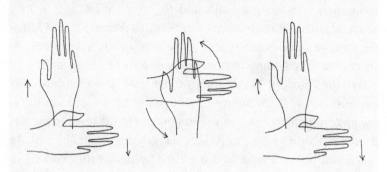

GAIA TOUCH EXERCISE TO EXPERIENCE THE PLANT CORE OF
THE BODY

1. Position both hands in front of your chest in such a way
   that one hand is directed upward, the other is positioned
   horizontally. The palms touch each other.

2. Then move the vertical hand upward, and the horizontal
   one downward.

3. This movement is immediately followed by the opposite
   one.

4. When the hands meet again in the front of the chest
   there is a little pause. During the pause the positions of
   the hands change, while the palms still touch each other.
   The previously horizontal hand turns now to the vertical
   position, and vice versa.

5. After the change is done, the hands move as before, one
   upward and the other downward simultaneously.

6. Go on with this movement for a while, and then give
   yourself enough time to tap into the experience.

Earth and the power of the solar light. Similarly, I can feel my
body built around a light channel that resonates on one end with
the watery nature of Gaia; on the other side, it is aligned with the
fiery core of the Sun. Between the poles, there is a constant rhythmical exchange of binary impulses running through my body,
which is holding my vital axis alive. A relevant symbol would
be the Tree of Life, with the human body as its trunk; it is rooted
deeply in the Earth, with its branches reaching toward the Sun.

The inspiration for the Gaia Touch exercise to experience the body suspended between the Earth and the Sun comes from a little town, Morro do Pilar, located in the Brazil's federal state of Minas Gerais. The town is positioned along a relatively steep slope. At its top there is a stony plateau connected to exquisite sources of interstellar powers. The bottom of the town sits in a bowl-like depression that is the source of a huge out-breath of vital forces coming from the core of Gaia. I was invited to the town to prepare a lithopuncture project to protect the geomantic qualities of the place, just before a large iron ore mine opened in its vicinity.

## The flute of Gaia

I cannot emphasize strongly enough how important it is at this moment in human evolution to reconnect with our plant-like essence. The plant within us might be the most ancient and also the most intimate path to connect the human essence to the heart of Gaia. I experience the light channel that I have just mentioned as a golden flute positioned along the backbone, understanding it as the backbone's causal dimension. In order to function as a musical instrument, like any flute, the "flute of Gaia" within each human body has little openings at various levels. The openings could be called the chakras of our plant body. I would say that there are five of them:

- The lowest one is located at the level of our sexual organs and is related to the primeval powers of Gaia.
- The second, at the level of the kidneys, is related to the life powers of Gaia.
- The third, at the level of the lungs, is related to the breath exchanged between the Earth and its parent star, the Sun.
- The fourth, at the level of the vocal cords, is related to the capacity to translate patterns from the causal world into the creative power of the word.
- The fifth, at the level of the ears and eyes, is related to the capacity of the human being for self-consciousness.

We shall expand our knowledge of the five levels of the flute of Gaia when observing the body's binary organs in the third part of our journey.

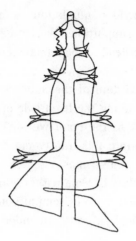

*The flute of Gaia*

To understand the function of our plant body, one can imagine Gaia constantly exchanging breath with the Sun, using the "flute" of the human body as her instrument. As an effect of the flow of the breath, different sounds are produced. Which sound resounds within the human being in a given moment depends on which of the five openings of the tube has been activated. When we move with our attention through the various layers of the daylight world before us, we press upon different holes of the flute to make the song of Gaia "audible" in the manifested world. If we peoples of the Earth would allow our plant-like body to function at its full potential, then the Earthly Cosmos would sound a thousand times stronger and sweeter than the best philharmonic orchestra.

I have seen that blocking the fantastic potential of the human being to function as the musical instrument of Gaia is the reason for certain adverse genetic interventions that were done in the past. The aim is obviously to eventually block the flute totally; the last time this was attempted, according to my insight, was during the Nazi regime. If people are cut off from their heritage of inhabiting the planet as daughters and sons of Gaia, the whole purpose of their existence as embodied beings is destroyed, and they become weak. As such, they are easy to manipulate by the forces challenging the course of human evolution and the evolution of the Earth.

As a result of genetic manipulations, a false pattern of Gaia's flute has developed, supporting the emergence of the alienated human personality. Instead of the human being centering its existence on the flute of Gaia—on the constant dialogue between Gaia and the solar wisdom of the Sun—a kind of by-pass has been created. It runs along the front side of the body, bypassing the basic human link to the plant world. The threat is that the human race will fall into this trap completely, consenting to its alienation from the Earth Cosmos.

To reactivate the flute of Gaia within your body I propose the following breathing exercise. To remind you: the breathing tube of Gaia is set up vertically through the middle of your body.

## *The feminine aspect of our plant body*

The masculine dimension of the plant world is clearly present in the vertical trunk of a tree or an upright blade of grass. The same is mirrored in our body, through our upright posture and backbone. The watery/feminine aspect of our plant body can be compared with the foliate organism of the forests or with the beauty and the scent of flowers. How unique are flowers in their colorful diversity! In the case of human beings, the same quality is revealed through the beauty of human bodies in the full spectrum of their different shades and shapes. The watery and plant-like qualities of our body inspire erotic relationships and the enjoyment of life.

Another important gift of our plant body is our quality of health. Plants are beings capable of offering help when we get ill in the form of direct plant preparations or in homeopathic form. It is time that human beings awaken to their plant nature, to enable an era where the plant's beauty and health find their home in the human body again.

GAIA TOUCH EXERCISE TO RENEW OUR PLANT-LIKE BODY

1. Stand or sit with the backbone upright. You are going to breathe through the separate holes of Gaia's flute within you.

2. Taking the first breath, imagine it coming from the core of the Earth, and lead it up to the level of your kidneys. A short pause follows while you are present here.

3. While breathing out, imagine pushing this breath of Gaia horizontally, partly forward, toward the manifested space in front of you, and partly backward, toward the liquid universe of the causal dimension.

4. Take the next breath, imagining it simultaneously partly from the space in front of you and partly from the back space, leading it to the same opening of the flute at the level of the kidneys. A short pause follows.

5. While breathing out, direct your breath upward toward the Sun.

6. Take the next breath imagining it coming from the heart of the Sun, and lead it down to the level of your kidneys, where a short pause follows. (It should be made clear here that not the fiery power of the Sun is inhaled, but the love of our parent star.)

7. While breathing out this breath of the Sun, imagine pushing it partly toward the causal world behind your back and partly to the front. (You are still at the level of the kidneys!)

8. Take the next breath simultaneously partly from the space behind your back and partly from the one in front of you. A short pause follows.

9. While breathing out, push the breath downward, imagine it going to the core of the Earth.

10. Now a cycle of breathing is finished. You can repeat it a few times. You can also decide to use another of the "holes" of the flute, as listed above.

4

# WE SHARE THE MIRACLE OF BEING ALIVE
# WITH THE ANIMAL KINGDOM

My relationship to animals changed radically last year when I was leading an Earth healing workshop in Kiel, northern Germany. I woke up in the middle of the night with the strange feeling that I had become a being altogether different from myself. Sitting up on the bed, fully awake, I tried to identify the being that I was feeling. It was a bear! I realized that I was sitting within the grand soft body of a bear.

The bear stood up and took a few steps away from my bed to show me a repulsive scene involving a magnificent stag. Demons had pushed the stag's body violently to the ground, so that I could feel the animal powerless and ruthlessly humiliated. The bear took the antlers from the stag's head and put them upon my head with the words: "You humans have knocked us to the ground, humiliating us. Yet we continue to live within you, proud of our creation."

I was sitting on the bed with the big antlers on my head, feeling like the Celtic god Cernunos . . .

*Animals are close relatives of the human race*

In effect, the scientific analysis of the human genetic code shows that we are 98 percent animal! The genetic difference between two species of chimpanzee is more then between the human being and animals. What the bear was proclaiming is true. Even if we cause the extinction of all the animal species on the Earth, they would continue to exist as a central part of our being. By enslaving animals and underestimating their spiritual role in the Earthly Cosmos we are suppressing a large part of our own being.

After I became aware of this deadly error, I was shown its consequence upon my body. I saw a thin wire tied around my body

*The manifested world and the "liquid" world of the causal dimension*

just above the solar plexus area. It was tied so tightly that I looked like an ant, almost divided into two parts. The dividing restriction seemed to be of ancient origin because the scar was grown over and could hardly be perceived. I felt a strong inner urge to bridge the gap separating me from my animal ancestors and to build a new and lasting bridge between my human self and myself as a member of the animal kingdom.

### The zodiac represents the cosmic status of animals

Modern civilization, attached to examining everything that matters in life with the methodology of reason, has collected a huge store of knowledge about animals and their existence. But the average selfish way of dealing with the natural environment is leading to the extinction of animal species and to ruthless exploitation. At the same time look at how many families who possess a cat, a dog, or a horse overload them with human love and care; and look at how many today are interested in the statements and revelations of astrology.

Why astrology? I mention astrology because this ancient knowledge about the zodiac hints that animals have a cosmic dimension that is usually ignored. The zodiac is basic for any astrological calculations. It is not by chance that most of the twelve constellations are symbolized by different animal species: the fish, the ram, the bull, the crab, the lion, the scorpion, the mountain goat. The name "zodiac" comes from the ancient Greek "zodiakos kyklos," meaning "the circle of animals."

It is likely that the whole zodiac was originally meant to be composed of animal symbols. The three human-like constellation symbols of Aquarius, the Twins, and the Virgin bear witness to the fact that human beings represent a part of the animal world.

To summarize, different animal species are an expression of corresponding universal archetypal patterns that are of cosmic origin. The zodiac, as was known by ancient cultures, is but a symbol, created by human culture to help understand the influences of the causal world upon our individual lives. Unfortunately, we have forgotten that the animals living in our surroundings are capable of embodying these cosmic patterns; and through them, enriching the vitality of our environment.

In the course of their evolution, in collaboration with Gaia and her helpers, animal species have created specific consciousness spheres (a kind of subtle vessels). Within these spheres, single animals, and individual human beings as well, can live out their lives. These consciousness spheres have different qualities, corresponding to the animal species that created them. They serve as vessels, containing important information needed for a being, animal, or human, to help them develop as an organism manifested in the form of a body.

My insight shows that before incarnation, human souls have to decide which animal's sphere or vessel they want to choose for the upcoming life span. The chosen animal vessel represents the archetypal pattern that our personal elemental being will use during the next step of the incarnation process for building our individual body.

Many ancient cultures knew the cosmic dimension of the animal kingdom and its deep influence upon the character and body-form of the human being. Egyptian gods, for example, were nearly all depicted with animal heads to make clear that their power and authority was based in the cosmic quality of the animal archetypes. The role of animal spirits in aboriginal cultures worldwide is another acknowledgment of the importance of the animal kingdom to our development.

## Animals are beyond the zoological dogmas

Plants are daughters of Gaia growing out of the Earth and her matrix. Complementary to the plants, one can imagine the animals as sons of the universe, coming to the Earth from above via their cosmic archetypes. Plants do not have inner organs; they project their vital functions outward into their environment. Leaves, flowers, and seeds are extended outward. Animals, on the contrary, developed the capacity to turn the bodily organs outside-in. Their vital organs—the heart, the digestion tract, the brain—as well as the capacity to breathe and to give birth to their offspring, were developed in inner spaces.

By creating inner organs, animals invented something fantastic, the freedom to move through the Earth's landscapes, a quality that human beings inherited from them—and have developed *ad absurdum*. Today we fly easily from one corner of the Earth to another, and we overload the world's motorways with traffic.

Among other gifts that we received from the animals I would like to emphasize three:

* Through the development of instincts, animals paved the way for our intuitions, and consequently, we are able to receive inspirations from earthly and cosmic sources. As beings of freedom, we need intuition in order to choose consciously the next steps on our path of development. This extraordinary gift makes it possible to know instinctively what is right and what is wrong.

* Animals developed the sense of togetherness in the flock or herd, leading to establishing communities. We have inherited this as the capacity to create families and communal networks, leading to founding and developing diverse cultures. Through our feeling for community, the jewel of unconditional love was discovered; love as a cosmic quality that now can be embodied, lived from day to day, and shared among all beings. A fantastic gift!

- Animals developed diverse techniques for absorbing the life force from Gaia and the Sun, manifesting it and moving it back and forth across the surface of the Earth, transforming it and distributing it among all living beings. Through this kind of combined effort of birds, insects, fish, reptiles, mammals, humans, etc., the life-force fields upon the Earth's surface are constantly refined, intensified, and shared. A precious service to life!

At one point, I had the privilege of slipping into the body of an animal, a deer, to activate the animal fully within me. What surprised me is the wide-awake nature of the animal. At each moment I felt to be jumping joyously, with my attention spread out over my environment. It was as if I were weaving a carpet of vivid colors. There was no limit to my astonishment. Each moment attracted me with its sweet power.

Animals are in constant communication with Gaia on one side and with their own natural ambience on the other. They receive the threads of life, only to pass them in the next moment to other living beings. They hold the weaving of life vibrant and present in each moment. Sadly, I was forced to realize that human beings are absent to this most of the time. Much of life's abundance is lost through their lack of attention to the flow of life.

To experience the animal presence within us I propose the following group exercise.

If you want to experience and deepen your personal relationship to your own animal body aspect within or to the animal world in general, you can perform the same two gestures at your own ear and nose. This will help to tap into your own animal aspects or contact animal beings around you. You can also invite an animal, with your imagination, to come onto your lap.

*The animal aspect of the human body*

I received a key on how to imagine the animal body of humans while I was waiting in Rome for a flight to the US. The flight was delayed, and I was a bit nervous from watching all the technicians moving around our plane, obviously not finding the problem. Suddenly I realized that the grey and red body of the airplane

GROUP EXERCISE DEDICATED TO OUR RELATIONSHIP WITH
THE ANIMAL WORLD

1. The group stands in a circle.

2. Our relationship with the animal world is affected through resonance with the four chakras of the animal body: two at the top of the ears, one at the tip of the nose, and the fourth at the end of the tail.

3. As the animal does not have our advanced individualization, our resonance with the animal world can be created by acting together as a group.

4. Each participant gently touches the uppermost crease of the ear of the person to the left. Gently rub the crease of the ear.

5. Simultaneously, participants rub the tip of their own nose with their index finger. At the tip of our nose there is also a chakra of our animal body aspect.

6. Be aware also of the chakra of our animal body that is located at the end of our imaginary tail. Imagine moving the tail back and forth.

7. After a certain time, change the direction of the rubbing of the ear tips from left to right.

resembled the body of a huge bird. In my imagination I started to caress it lovingly. I could feel its soft feathers under my fingers and see the flame of its bright eyes ready to move. In that instant the problem seemed to be settled, and we were invited to embark.

During the flight, I observed how a whole airplane "sits" comfortably inside a bird archetype, which provides the machine with the almost unerring capability to move through the air over great distances. I could feel the consciousness of the bird sharply focused upon the direction of our flight, and could feel its loving care for us passengers as if we were not just a herd of ignorant innocents.

In a similar way the animal body surrounds the human being as a consciousness sphere, as I described at the beginning of the chapter when I found myself inside a bear.

My experience tells me that human beings move inside a chosen animal throughout their life, usually not realizing its presence at all. It may appear as one's personal power animal, or it may have the characteristics of a zodiac sign or a clan totem. We are mostly too proud to admit that as embodied beings we are "children" of different animal species, finding excuses for denying it. (Later we will address the basic change going on presently in this relationship.)

The consciousness sphere of our personal animal surrounds and permeates our subtle body dimensions, holding us connected to the archetypal pattern and the quality of the chosen animal species. As a consequence we can have access to the above-mentioned gifts of the animal kingdom if we are open to accept them and to invite them to become active in our life.

On the other hand, their presence within our holon gives to the corresponding animal species the chance to take part in our human experiences. Through this, the animal species may receive impulses important for their further development.

While surrounding and permeating us, the sphere of our personal animal activates certain resonance points on our body. These serve as transmitters of various emotional and vital qualities of our personal animal, enabling us to absorb them. The following drawing shows where I perceive these points upon the human body. The rounded form in the middle of the human/animal chest relates to the space of the heart.

*Animal resonance points on the human body*

*Animals created conditions for the human heart system to manifest*

I have mentioned several wonderful gifts that we inherit from our animal relatives. Not to be overlooked is that animals "invented" the wonder of the heart, finally embodied as the physical organ within our chest; and so the possibility opened to develop our multidimensional heart system. Later, a special chapter will be dedicated to this theme.

I came to discover the hidden presence of the animal heart within the human body while exploring what I call "the universe of the heart." At some point, I noticed a black speck suspended near my physical heart, looking like an extinguished star. I thought its blackness might denote an aspect of the human heart constellation that presently is not active any more. Being interested in its original function, I dived with my intuition into the black star's history.

It turned out to be a relic of the animal heart within me. Its original quality I would compare with a tiny ball of amber. I understood the inherent message to be that in the course of evolution, leading human beings to greater steps of individuality, the animal heart within human beings has undergone various transmutations. Today I can perceive its precious presence as a kind of background of the human heart space.

By the heart space I mean the area between the throat and the belly. It is there where various "planets" (chakras) of our heart system (r)evolve around the "sun" of our heart center. I can see the transformed presence of the animal heart within the human being like a swarm of tiny stars representing the heart units descending from our animal ancestors. In their nano-form they constitute the background for the present-day human heart system, enabling it to work to its full potential.

# 5

# THE FAIRY ANCESTORS OF THE HUMAN RACE

Dear fellow traveler of the Gaia universe, in the present chapter we will continue to explore the constellations of the elemental world. I would remind you that in chapter 2 we touched upon the elemental kingdom while considering Gaia's creative hand—to be exact, her thumb. Working from the causal (back) side of the manifested world, Gaia's thumb takes care of the successful development of the four evolutions embodied upon the Earth. So that her thumb could perform its role, Gaia developed the multitude of elemental beings as holographic pieces of her consciousness, distributed over the surface of the Earth. Practically, it means that each plant, each river, each tree, each animal, each mountain, etc., during the time-span of its existence in the manifested world, is accompanied by a corresponding elemental being. Human beings are no exception.

## The elemental civilization of the Earth

Coming back to the theme of the elemental world, I need to underline that elemental beings represent only one facet of a much larger evolutionary sphere that has no name. It is often called "the fairy world," which is a bit confusing because fairies are considered to be elemental beings of the element of air. Yet in speaking of the fairy world, we should rather think of "the fairy-tale world."

It is a world composed of myriads of beings that were almost completely expelled from human awareness in the epoch of the expansion of several monotheistic religions whose leaders considered the Earth-related spirituality as competing with the Supreme Divinity—which is nonsense. If God is all-present, then why would God not also express through an innocent dwarf or a frog?

The second wave of suppression is (still today) fueled by the rational mind, which claims to not believe in dimensions of reality that cannot be touched physically, or logically proven. As a result, the fairy worlds, which at present do not have a physical form, are expelled into mythic realms or into books for children.

Working on my geomantic projects in many places in America and Europe, I find relics of the original civilization of the Earth. These relics are from the period before the human race started to intertwine with the fate of different worlds upon the Earth's surface. This was a time prior to the Neolithic age, which was when humanity developed its first civilization in the holon of the Earthly Cosmos, about ten millennia ago.

I can recognize the signs of this primary civilization. For example, I find gigantic stones positioned at sacred places in such a way that their cultural background is obvious, even though geologists declare them to be natural phenomena, and I encounter dolmens and other megalithic structures so enormous that ancient human communities could not have built them.

With their perfect synchronicity with the elements, along with their ability to channel the ideas and powers of their "mother," Gaia, the original civilization did not need any tools. They built, so to say, "from the inside," similar to Gaia creating geographic reliefs, butterflies, or landscapes. This is the reason why is it difficult to distinguish their creations from ones called "natural." A decade ago I discovered an example, a complex of pyramids at Visoko, near Sarajevo, at the core of the Balkans. Covered with woods and meadows, the pyramids look like unusually shaped mountains. And yet, analysis of the blocks from which they are built proves that they are made from an unusually strong natural concrete.

These megalithic monuments as well as many myths and legends give testimony of the existence of this elemental civilization of Earth, whose creators are known in the Irish-Celtic tradition as "Sidhe" (pronounced "She"). In old tales from the Tyrolean Dolomites they are called "Fanes." In the south of Germany, close to Bayreuth, where there are large monuments as testimony of their presence (like the Luisenburg Rock Labyrinth), I discovered the name "Erda," which in German means "those of the Earth." Another name appearing in German is "die Säligen" ("the blessed ones"). Since the name Sidhe is already used by John Matthews and my friend David Spangler, in order to identify them as beings of the fairy civilization in their present role, I will use the same name.

## Our fairy ancestors

Certainly, a period existed in the history of humanity when human culture cooperated with the parallel fairy evolution. In some places, as in the vicinity of Boulder, Colorado, or the previously-mentioned Luisenburg Rock Labyrinth, I found large stone installations that were obviously used as places of initiation. The human population would go there to be initiated into the secrets of how to live their life individually and as a community in harmony with the different extensions of the Earthly Cosmos and its beings. They would learn to connect especially with their own fairy-like heritage, with those facets of their body that have their origin in the fairy world.

What happened to the long-lasting cooperation between Sidhe and the human race? According to John Matthews' conversation with Sidhe a few years ago, humans became arrogant, dominating the planet. The community of Sidhe that originally was manifested and visible in their etheric bodies had to gradually withdraw into the invisible realms of the Earth's causal worlds.

According to Matthew, after realizing that the human race is about to destroy our common home, this wonderful planet Earth, Sidhe have the intention of re-appearing from their exile. They wish to offer their cooperation in the efforts to save the Earthly Cosmos from extinction.

To have an experience of the subtle quality of the Sidhe folk I can propose the following Gaia Touch exercise. It can only be done in groups. It should enable an experience of the group character of the fairy world and of the three levels constituting their cosmos:

- The so-called "middle world" is the core area of the Sidhe world, centered around their activities in the Earthly Cosmos.
- The "upper world" is the abode of the ancestors, the spiritual masters, of the fairy world.
- The "underground" dimension is the place similar to our monasteries, where the wisdom of Sidhe is stored, studied, and lived.

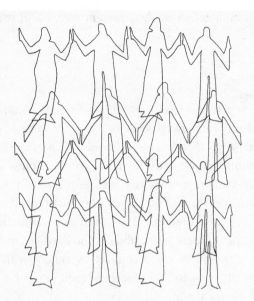

## GROUP RITUAL TO RELATE TO THE FAIRY WORLD

1. The group stands in a circle. The participants should touch each other by bringing the palms of their hands together in a very sensitive way.

2. First, keep the hands together at the level of your shoulders. This represents connection with the middle world.

3. Stay in an upright position and turn the hands; still touching, move them downward, so that the finger tips point to the center of the Earth. In this way, the contact to the sphere of the Sidhe underworld is created.

4. After some time, turn the hands and solemnly move them upward, still touching, and rest for a while in the middle world, as in step 2.

5. Afterward, move the hands, still touching, up as high as possible in order to get in contact with the upper world. In this way, the crown of the fairy world will be erected.

6. Now get again into contact with the middle world. During the whole ceremony, stay standing upright in the axis of your body.

7. In order to finish this group ritual, you can either clap your hands for a short while against the hands of your neighbors to honor the group character of the fairy world ... or

8. If you want to experience the newly created relationship with the fairy world of Gaia, it is better to dissolve the circle in silence. Participants should take some time to feel its specific quality.

## The elemental self of the human being

Before we start to explore the relationship between the fairy world and the human race, it needs to be stated that the concept that declares the human being is a "spiritual entity" inhabiting an earthly body for the time span of our incarnation upon Earth, is a wrong concept. The image of dressing in robes just before birth and the removing of the robes on death is an anthropocentric trick to hide from us the great treasure that we potentially inherit since the remote time when Gaia invited us humans to take part in the evolution of the Earthly Cosmos. By treasure, I mean our birthright to experience ourselves as proper beings of the Earth like the animals, oceans, mountains, or plants.

This might represent little value to people as long as they are not interested in any deep relationship to Gaia and do not realize that this planet is a living and breathing Book of Life, a jewel of creation. Perhaps only when looking back to the Earth after having died, they may feel sorrow, realizing that they have missed something extremely valuable.

Practically, it means that Gaia, the Mother of Life, offers to each of us humans the unique opportunity to develop a special aspect of our identity, closely related to the essence of the Earth. To give it a name, my daughter Ajra, invented the concept of the "elemental self," meaning our own elemental identity. I myself met my own elemental self for the first time in a dream:

*I am a boy hiding alone in a bunker, proud of the fact that nobody can find me. Outside, the bunker is overgrown with climbing plants. A round breathing hole is the only connection with the outer world. I approach the hole to look out into the world. In that same moment the face of a boy, identical to mine, looks through the same hole into my hiding place. Because outside the bunker is overgrown with plants, his face appears garlanded with green leaves.*

The boy hiding in the bunker represents the personality of the contemporary human being caught in its own narrow world. The second boy appears as if indicating the possible way out. Since he is garlanded with green leaves, he obviously represents that aspect of myself that is part of the elemental world. I have met my elemental self.

The image of the two brother-boys, addresses the elemental self as complementary to our human identity. While our human identity relates to the matrix of the human race, the elemental self is something completely different. The elemental self enables us to become integrated into the larger community of life, to take on our role as part of Gaia's creative hand. It is not something temporal, related only to a specific life span spent on Earth. It is rather a value that enriches our being beyond space and time limitations, and also beyond the epoch, while we take part in the evolution of the Earthly Cosmos.

By working continuously from incarnation to incarnation on developing our elemental identity, as human beings we grow toward becoming individual co-creators with Gaia, taking over the role predicted by the air element finger of Gaia's creative hand. She needs our conscious cooperation now, in this epoch of great changes, and will need it even more in the future, when the Earth Soul intends to unfold all the unpredictable potentials of the Earthly Cosmos to their full beauty and perfection.

I propose a Gaia Touch exercise to achieve a personal experience of your identity as a member of the elemental aspect of Earth evolution.

### Sidhe as a parallel to human evolution

Before we look for the fairy layers within the tissues of our own body, we need to be aware that the fairy-kind of body is not attached to any fixed form — This is a characteristic that applies to all beings of the elemental worlds. Such a body can easily change its form in order to reflect a specific function to be performed in the geomantic environment. It can mirror the evolutionary step that individual beings or groups of beings have achieved on the path of their development; as well as be a reflection of certain cultural patterns invented by the local folklore to serve as a key to recognizing the fairy beings present in their environment. The appearance of a fairy body can even change in

EXERCISE TO CONNECT WITH THE PERSONAL ELEMENTAL
BEING AND THE ELEMENTAL SELF

1. Fold your hands in the prayer gesture and reach above your
   head backward toward the point on your backbone located
   between the shoulder blades. This is the focus of our elemental self. Human beings resonate here with the essence of
   themselves as elemental (fairy-like) beings of Gaia.

2. Go with the prayer gesture across the central axis of the head
   and the body down to the level of your heart, keeping in
   touch with your face and body all the time. Pause at the heart
   center to bless your fairy essence with the love of your heart.

3. Staying there, turn the prayer gesture upside down to touch
   with the fingertips the solar plexus area as the focus of the
   personal elemental being.

4. After a short pause, perform a rounded gesture above your
   head to declare yourself as a member of the large circle of
   Gaia's elemental family.

the moment, if needed, as a vehicle to convey a certain message
to the observer.

To present-time human imagination the fairy worlds are
immersed in the withdrawn state of invisibility (the unreachable
condition of invisible existence). It is important to underline that
this is not their natural state of presence, but a result of millennia

long pressure from human cultures pushing those worlds into a kind of exile. As already mentioned, this tragic situation is changing today as an effect of the Earth's transmuting process. More and more people are now opening their minds and hearts to the subtle realms of the Earthly Cosmos, which enables the forced-out beings, like Sidhe, to come closer to manifested reality again.

The first step in our re-connection with the parallel evolution of Sidhe might be to accept the notion that we as human beings are close relatives of the fairy world. Since our evolutions were closely coupled in the past, in a way, we share the same ancestral line. This means that the human race—each one of us individually—could reconnect and call to life from one's own inner world the noble qualities that distinguish the fairy world from the average behavior of the modern-day human being. Let me mention some of them:

- Sidhe civilization does not know anything but truth. This means that the natural status of their mind is to be true to their essence. Reconnecting with the legacy of our fairy relatives means to detach from our habitual superficiality and to become again a race devoted to truth. I do not mean only truth in the mental sense of the word, but also in the sense of living our lives truthfully.

- Sidhe civilization does not know anything but harmony. It is time for the human race to learn to co-exist and be creative without continuously producing conflicting situations. We seem to need to cheat ourselves with the illusion that as beings of free will we can do whatever we want, no matter how destructive it is.

- Sidhe civilization—and this is valid for all the elemental worlds of the Earth—does not know past or future. They know only the fullness of the present moment in which past and future are contained. For human beings, who most of the time get lost in thoughts concerning the no-longer existing past or the not-yet existing future, this is an inspiration to learn again to be focused in the present moment and to be aware of its limitless potentials.

## The subtle fairy body hidden within the human figure

I have several times observed groups of Sidhe beings (Fanes, Erda, Säligen) cautiously approaching our human world, and by this, revealing the form of their existence. Their body consistency can be best described as watery based, yet combined with the colorful light of the fire element. The watery quality of their bodies displays its basic difference from angelic beings, which are primarily beings of light. The water quality is denser then pure light, which brings the fairy body closer to material reality.

My perceptions show that our forgotten subtle fairy body is still present in the background of our physical body, but compressed into its tissue matter so that it can hardly be perceived. Further I believe that Sidhe, as the primeval civilization of the Earth, donated to us humans our first body so that we would be able to walk and develop upon this beautiful planet—we are relating here to the epoch known in our myths as the time of the Paradise. Only later, with the help of the parallel evolutions of plants, minerals, and the animal community, our body became denser and finally materialized.

To remember the Sidhe layer of our own body and to again appreciate it, I will share with you my perceptions of its main features. To be clear, this is not a representation of the fairy body by itself, but an attempt to show its traces within the human organism:

- One of the purposes of the fairy body is to enhance human creativity within the Earthly Universe; this is why its throat area is enlarged as a broad energy field. It supports our capacity to create through the medium of the word.
- Its basic creative organs are positioned between the base of the throat and the root of the nose, where the fairy third eye is focused. This enables the human being insights into the causal dimensions of reality.
- The third element of the fairy body is integrated into the human hands, and connected to the role of the throat and the tongue. Its function is to lead creative visions toward their manifestation in living reality. When integrated into the human hands,

this fairy quality enables our hands to be moved by the patterns of the causal world as we use them for work.

- Inside the intersection of both major energy fields of the Sidhe body, I can perceive the powerful point of the elemental heart connecting them to the present moment in time and space. The elemental heart offers to human beings the possibility of always connecting to the present moment of Gaia's time and space rhythms.

- The fairy head, resonating with the human brain cavity, has a kind of large ears rounded up like shells that function as antennas that enable us to think together with the universal noosphere. In this way, besides using the individual "library" of the brain, human beings can think also in tune with the pool of universal wisdom.

- The realm of the belly (pelvic cavity) has a different use in the Sidhe body than in ours. The individual holon of the being takes a knot-like turn around, connecting it directly with the causal realms of Gaia, which in this case means a free entrance to the memory stored within the belly of the Earth—including the knowledge of how to create using Gaia's primeval powers.

- The influence of the Sidhe body related to our feet is also of importance. The lower part of our fairy body is designed as a kind of sail that enables us to move along the subtle dimensions of the manifested world. When we are able to awaken this quality within our legs, we will cease needing mechanical transportation.

In the present epoch of Earth's transmutation it is of great importance to become aware of the Sidhe dimension of our human body. It can help us reach that level of transparency that we need to connect to the multidimensional features of the newly constituting space and time structure.

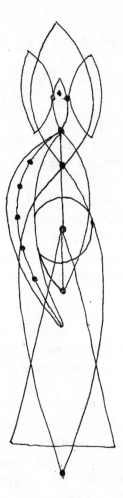

*How to imagine the elements of the fairy body as distributed throughout the human organism*

# 6

# THE HUMAN BEING MANIFESTED

Dear companion on the path through the integral human body! For clarity sake, I wish to summarize briefly the path we have traveled along the horizontal arm of our compass, the spherical cross. We have traveled till now through the three layers of the causal world at the back-space of the human body:

- The human being in its plant-like aspect—represents our identity as a being of the Earth, rooted in its core.
- The human being in its animal-like aspect—represents the basis for us to become present, attentive, and community-orientated beings.
- The human being as a close relative of the fairy world — represents our capacity to exist as creative embodied beings in the environment of the Earth planet.

To proceed on our path in a balanced way we need now to focus our attention to the other side of the horizontal arm of our key archetype, toward the layers of the manifested world extending in front of our face. In the next three chapters we will be turning around our own human identity. The human status that we explored before now turns upside down:

- The human being's identity is not only plant-like. Plants play an important role in our causal world, but the human being knows also its own identity.
- The human being is not only a fairy being. Even though closely related to the elemental world, the human being is a being evolving around the human archetype.
- The human being is not only a being of nature. Even if closely related to the worlds of plants and animals, and a member of the living organism of the Earth, the human being is also capable of creating cultural structures.

In the next steps of our exploration we have to temporarily leave the worlds of plants, animals, and elemental beings that exist parallel (synchronic) to ours, and focus specifically on our

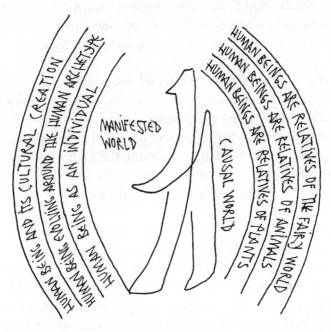

*The three layers of the manifested world in relation to the causal*
*dimensions — all in relationship to the human being*

human characteristics among the beings of the Earthly Cosmos.
This includes the cultural aspects of the human world.

## The binary rhythm of the human presence in the Earthly Cosmos

Our attention until now has been dedicated to the relationship
between the human race and other evolutions with important
roles to play in the human body. Now we need to look upon the
human race as a rounded-up sphere with its own characteristics
and purpose. But, if we are ready to look upon the human world
as one of the autonomous spheres of the Earthly Cosmos, then
we need to take into account its binary rhythm, composed of the
exchanging rhythms of the causal and manifested dimensions.
As with animals, plants, and landscapes, human beings are not
limited to their material appearance in the everyday world.

Besides being present in the daily world under the bright
light of the Sun, the human race also has its own realms of the

causal world called "the world of ancestors and descendents." In the sense of the binary rhythm, we can speak of two constantly exchanging phases of existence, the archetypal (causal) and the manifested (embodied) one.

During the archetypal phase, we abide within the ambience of a causal (non-manifested) world, a subtle kind of world representing the home and evolutionary environment of those human beings who are not in embodiment at a given moment, the ancestors, who at the same time represent the future children, "the descendents." As beings woven out of light substance, we abide within one of the worlds that exists parallel to the manifested realm of the Earth.

In its second phase, the human being enters the dimension of the manifested world through the gate of birth in order to spend a specific time span within the embodied Earth dimension among plants, animals, landscapes, minerals, human companions, and elemental beings. After the given life span is concluded, we detach again from the manifested world level to continue our existence in the archetypal dimension.

The binary cycle of incarnation runs parallel to the daily cycle of being awake and asleep. The period of sleep can be compared with the phase of abiding within the world of the ancestors and descendents. The period of awakeness and perceiving the world of forms is comparable to the phase when the soul develops its presence within the manifested dimension of the Earthly Cosmos.

Related to the binary code of human existence, it needs to be underlined that the sphere of the archetypal world is not positioned somewhere else in the cosmos, but exists right here where the sphere of our touchable daylight world vibrates. It is only that the world of the ancestors and descendents exists at a different frequency level. Our dear deceased, who at the same time are the future children, exist as subtle entities all around us, some closer, some further away, but we can not see or touch them because of the vibrational difference.

Here is a relevant Gaia Touch cosmogram:

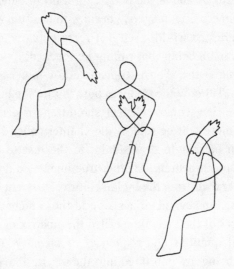

GAIA TOUCH EXERCISE TO CONNECT WITH THE WORLD OF
ANCESTORS AND DESCENDENTS

1. Reach with your hands into the space behind your back, and
   at the same time tilt your head backward as much as possible. You should feel that your tilted head is aligned with
   your hands. By this you have found the key to contact the
   world of ancestors and descendents.

2. Then transfer your hands to your chest, crossed to bless the
   contact with the love of your heart.

3. The exercise should be concluded with the gesture of ado-
   ration dedicated to the world of ancestors and descendents.
   Your head is tilted forward. Your hands are lifted above
   your head, positioned parallel to each other, with the palms
   directed to the back space.

4. After the exercise is repeated a few times, you should listen
   to its message.

## The soul as a focus of common human identity

Often when pondering about the essence of the human being, the
concept of "the soul" is used. But before integrating the concept
of the soul into the framework of our journey, we need to detach
from the traditional opinion about the nature of the soul, that of

positioning it above the body as a kind of ruler. To liberate the soul from esoteric imagery, I decided to position it in the realms of the manifested world, even if it represents one of the extensions of the human being that cannot be touched.

Through the Earth transmutation process, the situation changes. Till now the soul was pushed into the human back space. Now the time comes when it should again permeate the whole body—more will be said in the chapter called Intermezzo I. The soul can be imagined as similar to the rosette on the facade of the Gothic cathedrals. Another true image would be a light mandala as known from the Indian culture. Different colorful imprints positioned in several circles around the center represent different sequences of the archetype called the "matrix of the soul." All the different qualities and sequences of memory that represent the human being are imprinted into the rosette-like pattern.

Yet the rosette of the soul should not be imagined as a mere journal of memories. The mandala of the soul is not only a geometric pattern, but also a being. Some philosophies call it "the higher self of the human being." But such a hierarchical status does not correspond to the essence of the soul. The expression "higher" has to be changed to "common." All the qualities that are common to human beings are coded in the matrix of the soul.

If the sphere of an individual soul opens in front of me like a shell, then it is clear to me that it contains something very precious. This precious thing is carefully folded together like a butterfly in a cocoon. I used to call it the matrix of the perfected human self. It contains all the potentials that enable human beings to develop along innumerable different pathways. Seen from another point of view, the rosette of the soul contains all the human potentials that can be activated by any human individual at any time if feeling, thinking, and acting in accordance with one's true self. They are stored in the sphere of the soul like in a seed.

When addressing the issue of the soul, we think of the archetype (matrix) of the human being as valid for all of us members of the human race, regardless of the color of our skin, or our ideological or religious orientation, etc. Beyond the binary rhythm of the individual human cycling between the world of the ancestors and the manifested dimension exists the matrix of the human soul as a reminder that we are not only individuals subject to our own will and purpose, but also members of a wide community called humankind.

Further, the matrix of the soul is not exclusively bound to the era of human evolution within the Earthly Cosmos. Within its rosette are also coded experiences of human history, coupled with other star systems, collected in the epochs before Gaia called us to join her creative process in transforming "her" planet into an earthly paradise garden.

## The human being on its way toward embodiment

On its way toward embodiment, the human being as a being of subtle nature has to collaborate with the elemental (Gaia-related) beings to create the power field and the forms of existence within which its presence in the world of matter and in the circumstances of daily life can take place. While existing in our archetypal phase, human beings are free of any preconceived form. They can appear as geometrical or colored light patterns. We are also free to take on a form inherited from one of our previous incarnations. But upon stepping onto the path of embodiment, the human being needs proper conditions in order to be able to appear in the time and space framework, and that demands relatively fixed forms.

The soul starts to approach the embodied world long before it appears as an embryo in the mother's womb. My intention is to describe the path toward incarnation based upon my experiences of two landscapes in Europe that serve as a path for incarnating human beings approaching material reality. Ancient cultures recognized the essential importance of such landscapes, and marked these places related to different phases of incarnation as sacred places. This enabled me to explore more in detail the soul's path while approaching its future body. One of those landscapes can be found in the Alpine region of Germany (Oberallgäu), the other one, in the mountainous center of France, is called the Massif Central.

Let me briefly share my experiences concerning the phases of the soul's path toward its embodiment.

The consciousness of water offers the first possibility to the future child when stepping down toward embodiment. The noosphere of water, due to its high grade of sensitivity, enables the soul to make its first imprint in the manifested world. This imprint has, in effect, the quality of "information only." One can imagine it practically as an imprint of the incoming soul within the water body (emotional body) of the future mother.

The archetypal powers of the elements of fire, water, earth, and air make the second step of individual's approach to the manifested world possible by holding upright the bridge between the causal and manifested worlds. Thus a multidimensional energy field is being created as a precondition for the incoming being to embody. During this phase the incoming child experiences the first contact with the vital-energy dimension of the embodied world.

Also the third step has to be accomplished before conception and the following pregnancy in the mother's womb takes place. At this stage the incarnating human being meets the world of the fairy beings and "falls in love" with a particular elemental being. To say it more exactly, the incoming human individual and the chosen elemental being sign a contract about their common future. It is a kind of marriage between them. The chosen elemental being will accompany and help its human complement throughout the whole lifetime to master the challenges of the manifested world. From this moment on the two will abide within the same "house" (later more about this mainly neglected situation).

Simultaneously, the collaboration of the incoming child with the animal kingdom takes place. As already mentioned, throughout their evolution animals have created models of different characters as preconditions for the bodily forms to be developed. The soul has to choose a particular model to step through into the incarnated body. With the help of the day and hour of birth, astrology is capable of clarifying which model was chosen by the individual, and with it, its specific qualities and inherent tasks for the future life.

Now the incoming human being has all the conditions ready to develop as an embryo within the mother's womb. During the

### GAIA TOUCH EXERCISE TO IDENTIFY WITH YOUR INDIVIDUAL SOUL MATRIX

1. Lay down on your back with your body stretched out and enter your inner peace. Imagine slipping backward into the Earth — as a sphere of consciousness the inside of the Earth can be approached at any time.

2. After arriving inside the Earth, you should position yourself inside a kind of mold directly beneath you. This mold at the center of your "rosette" represents the matrix of your being. It is made of liquid minerals in the form that corresponds exactly to the features of your body.

3. Ask beings that are helping you in your development to complement the mold with those aspects of your archetype that are beyond your capacity to imagine. Take time to reconnect with your matrix.

4. At the proper moment you should return back to your presence here and now; yet staying rooted in the archetype beneath. Memorize the experience. Give thanks.

period of pregnancy the co-creative role of the mineral kingdom comes into its place. By incorporating fine mineral particles into the body of the embryo, a properly embodied human being comes into existence who is capable of entering the manifested world through the door of birth.

The next Gaia Touch exercise is designed to help the individual to re-connect with his or her individual matrix. The experience is possible through relating to the imprint of the soul's archetype stored within the memory of the Earth. When lying down on your back, the matrix can be experienced as positioned directly under the body.

The exercise can be used as part of a daily meditative practice. It can also be used in the times of possibly difficult planetary changes, when the stability or security of our lives is endangered. In this case, it works as an exercise of personal attunement or protection. While anchored in the individual matrix belonging to the wealth of Gaia's life codes, one is safe.

## The soul's window into infinity

Imagining the matrix of the human soul as a rosette. There are many colored windows within its composition that could be opened, and their treasure revealed. We have just opened one of them relating to our common archetype as human beings. Relating to the binary rhythm of the soul, we touched upon the individual aspects of the soul. Furthermore, we should not forget to open another window, the soul's window into infinity, connecting us as human beings with our divine parents. Without their presence, it would be not possible for any of the evolutions involved to appear within the Earthly Cosmos, to develop in the exquisite conditions of its holon, to enjoy the gifts of the embodied life, and to create in the conditions of matter.

When I speak about our divine parents, I have in mind the intimate relationship between the Earth and her partner the Sun. I do not wish to superimpose here the classical father-mother relationship. Like the Earth, the Sun is luckily also of feminine nature, at least in the German language. Yet it is obvious that the watery ambience of the Earth and the fiery face of the Sun complement each other in an ideal way. The Earth's purpose is to generate countless forms of life, while the Sun, with its heat and light, is to create a cosmic environment in which all of us manifested beings can develop and rejoice at the beauty of life.

MEDITATION TO EXPERIENCE OUR RELATIONSHIP
AS HUMAN BEINGS WITH THE DIVINE PARENTS OF
THE EARTHLY COSMOS

1. Imagine us, the human family (and possibly also groups of other beings) sitting in circles around the Earth. The Earth is positioned at the center. Build a loving relationship from your heart to the core of Gaia.

2. Now imagine the bright point of the Sun positioned behind your back at approximately the same level. Imagine its proper distance from the back of your heart, but have in mind the quality of infinity.

3. Now attune yourself to the presence of both "parents," the Earth at the center of the Earthly Cosmos and the Sun behind your back at the farthest point of the horizon. Find the center within the area of your chest where you can relate at this moment in an optimal way to both "parents."

4. If you then imagine all of us beings of Gaia sitting in circles around the core of the Earth, with the Sun moving graciously at a distance around the Earth and our circles, you will understand why the ancient cultures always thought in the framework of a geocentric world system.

To experience the double presence of divinity through body movements I can propose a Gaia Touch exercise that was inspired by the ancestors of the Bogomils in Bosnia. It appeared in my consciousness when visiting the Bogomil necropolis at Radimlja (Radimlja is located near Stolac, Bosnia and Herzegovina). Standing beside a "stečak"—a kind of Bogomil graveyard stone—my hands were lifted to form a cross and then folded inwardly. At the same time I heard a voice saying, "the Christ is within you." Bogomils, as a religious movement parallel to the medieval Cathars, denied the right of the Christian Church to represent Christ in the form of an institution. They summoned people to find the integral divinity within them, at the core of their own heart.

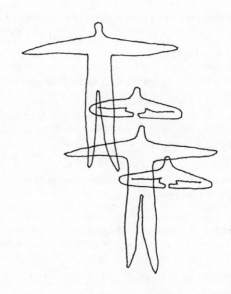

BOGOMIL GESTURE TO EXPERIENCE DIVINITY AT THE CENTER
OF YOUR BEING

1. Stretch out your arms to both sides, so that your body shows
   the form of a cross. Imagine embracing the whole universe
   through this gesture.

2. Bend your arms at your elbows so that your palms come to
   rest on your chest.

3. Become aware that the divinity is not only vibrating through
   the widths of the universe, but also is present in the space of
   your heart. Feel this quality inside.

4. Repeat the gesture a few times to deepen the experience.

# 7

# CAN THE EGO BE CONSIDERED AS SOMEBODY?

Relating to the five fingers of Gaia's creative hand, dear co-traveler, we have touched upon her forefinger and the middle finger (the worlds of plants and animals). We then jumped to Gaia's thumb to visit the world of the fairy and elemental beings. With the last chapter we started to dive into the secrets of the human being—Gaia's smallest finger. Relating to the human being in the last chapter, first of all, the three layers of our causal dimension had to be considered. The present chapter is different in its orientation, facing those dimensions that enable the human being to be active in the manifested world. Usually these are in connection with the human personality or ego.

## The limitless spectrum of human roles

At the moment human beings step out of the causal dimensions and enter the manifested world, they have to choose a certain role. Before stepping out the door one needs to put on shoes, a coat, and a "mask" — whether being a mother in a family, a master behind a machine, a child in the sandbox, a soldier on a battlefield, an official behind a desk, and so forth. And in a lifetime we are often jumping from one role to another. Is it the destiny of the human being to wander for a whole life from one role to another? To be able to answer this question, one needs first to feel what it means to be a human being and migrate continually from one role to another.

The result of pondering this question is rather crushing. If a human being fully submits to different roles, he or she ceases to exist as a human. Instead, I see the personality appear like a snail rolled-in around itself. Here we should speak of the three causes of the egocentric personality:
- The emptied ego comes about when one renounces one's creative essence.

- The emptied ego comes about when one detaches from one's causal dimensions—presented in the last chapter as the binary rhythm of the human family, the connection to the human matrix, and the connection to the divine dimensions of the Earthly Cosmos.
- The emptied ego also comes about if one forgets oneself as a being of freedom.

It is possible to turn the negative sides of the egocentric personality around and present them as something positive. The term "ego" comes from the Latin "I am," which lets us know that we are dealing here with an aspect of human identity that can be of good use when entering the manifested world. But before considering the diverse potentials of the human personality, I wish to propose next a Gaia Touch exercise to work on transforming the alienated ego.

## The human being as a being of freedom

It is not easy to understand the logic behind Gaia's decision to allow humans, as beings of freedom, to settle in her planetary garden. The Earth existed as a relatively harmonious place in the solar system before human beings began to implement their "free will," which can be labeled rather as "self-will" ("Relatively harmonious" means that the power of transmutation was always integrated as an agent of change.). Since the human race started to implement its self-will about five millennia ago, we have witnessed an uninterrupted chain of wars, destruction of the biosphere of the Earth, suppression of fellow beings of the nature kingdoms, etc.

It needs to be acknowledged that at the same time, the creative capacities of the free human being are precious and necessary for the evolution of the Earthly Cosmos:

- Humans as beings of freedom are capable of loving their fellow beings out of the autonomous decision of their own hearts, without necessarily having to be required to do so by the angelic or other beings of the Earth or universe.
- Such free individuals are able to create out of their own inspiration without leaning upon the guidance of beings who know

## GAIA TOUCH EXERCISE TO TRANSFORM THE ALIENATED PERSONALITY

1. While sitting, with your thumb and middle finger you should symbolically break off from your solar plexus a bit of your ego substance. In the modern human being, the energy cloud of the alienated personality is usually attached to the emotional surface of the plexus area.

2. Now carry the bit of ego substance up toward your heart center and touch the center with it. You will see the bit of your ego, while touching your heart space, light up like a tiny star.

3. In your imagination the star starts to move through your body in the direction of your back space, and then down toward the coccyx. Hold your hands at the coccyx to catch the star when it settles down.

4. Imagine that at the base of your back the creative hand of Gaia touches your hands. The encounter makes the ego awaken to the need to abolish the egocentric aspect of its will and to listen to the inspiration of Gaia, the Mother of Life.

5. The power of the renewed synergy between Gaia and the human self pushes the renewed personality pattern through the body onto your lap.

6. Simultaneously, lay your hands on your lap, feeling like a mother holding a newborn baby—your personality attuned to the essence of life.

and hold close the already existing patterns of creation. This results in inventions in the realm of life and culture that have not been thought of before in the universe.

• Existing as free individuals, human beings can care for the diverse beings and aspects of the Earthly Cosmos outside of their obligation to the rules of behavior settled by human standards. Such acts of care bring more joy and fulfillment to all involved because they are deliberate acts of individual dedication.

For the personality to achieve such a high state of responsibility two polarized sets of experiences are needed. On one hand, the human ego has to experience the consequences of its self-will upon the personal or even collective level. To say it in a symbolic way, an ego often needs to go down to the deepest hell to experience how it feels when the precious gift of freedom is used for destructive purposes.

On the other hand, possibilities are offered to the human being continuously by the stream of life to experience the enriching results of the decision to use the gift of freedom in a creative way. Such experiences show how one's own life and the lives of companion beings are enriched if the gift of free will is being used in a responsible and loving manner.

## The human being and the art of life

It is true that humans often behave like madmen, raving through the world as crazed destroyers. Yet we are also capable of developing deeply touching expressions through different venues of creativity, especially in the field of art. From the astonishing beauty of Paleolithic animal images in caves like Altamira in Northern Spain to the modern, abstract paintings of Kandinsky, we can marvel at the uninterrupted continuity of human creative achievements. The gift of our free decision, coupled with our capacity to think in an autonomous (logical) way, opens to human beings a favorable prospective for our existence and creativity within the Earthly Cosmos.

The gift to be free in our creative endeavors enables our collaboration with the muses to bring forth unprecedented results. To put it in a poetic way, the muses are the daughters of Gaia. They relate to a specific aspect of Gaia consciousness capable of generating creative ideas. The muses are able to transform these ideas into inspirations that can reach the threshold of human intuitive awareness. Yet the field of activity that muses cover is by no means restricted to the different forms of art, but encompasses also other realms of life.

The gift of freedom is also a prerequisite for our autonomous heart system to come into existence. It is similar to a micro-constellation composed of different star-like centers. This concept will be considered in depth during the third part of our journey through the extensions of the human universe.

Finally, I believe that creative freedom was offered to human beings to enable us to become conscious collaborators with Gaia's creative hand. Our capacity to create through the synergy between our hands, body, and imagination is of decisive importance in this respect.

Herewith our exploration of the smallest finger of Gaia's creative hand is concluded. The smallest finger is allotted to the human race perhaps to remind us how senseless it is to rise above other beings of the Earthly Cosmos to try to rule over them. Unfortunately, the human race has misused the gift of free will, plunging itself into exactly that stupidity. We can only hope that the consequences will be accompanied by a high level of divine mercy.

# 8
# THE MARVEL OF MATTER

Reflecting briefly on what has been covered so far, you will realize, dear co-traveler, that there is still one of the five fingers of Gaia's creative hand that we have yet to consider. It is the ring finger, representing the earth element, and related to the world of minerals. This is the last, yet, I believe this is not a mistake. On the contrary, it makes sense, since the role of the mineral kingdom is to bring about the densest form of existence called "matter." It is the last to come into focus if we are moving from the causal world toward embodiment, or toward the densest form of manifestation concerning the human body and the body of the Earth.

## *The lithosphere at the base of the world of form*

In the Prologue, I voiced my resistance concerning the image of the Earth as a ball of dense matter, an image that constantly infiltrates our rational minds. Now, at the end of our journey through the "middle world," I must say that this dense sphere of matter is a jewel of Gaia's creation.

Looking through the eyes of the earth element, the manifested world is composed of an infinite multitude of fine particles of matter, altogether constituting a rounded-up sphere called a "lithosphere" in Greek, "a sphere composed of stones." The name is used to address the thick layer of minerals upon which the materialized body of Earth's landscapes is sitting. From that mineral foundation, minute particles of minerals are constantly being "sucked" onto the manifested level of reality. At each moment, they give the needed consistency to the materialized world of nature and culture that extends all around us.

Following the analogy between the landscape and the human organism, the question arises — Is it the lithosphere that gives the human body the quality of something that can be seen, touched, and embraced?

To answer the question, a possible misunderstanding must be clarified. I mean the idea from the rational mind that mineral substance must be stiff and hard. How is it then possible that the human body appears as a living, thinking, and breathing organism even though it incorporates a dimension that is identified with stiff mineral substance?

The materialized human body, even if composed of mineral particles, can move as a living organism because it cooperates with the other three of the four elements. Practically, I mean the interaction of the human lithosphere with the water body, with certain aspects of the fire body, and the noosphere of the air element. Their interaction forms the reality we see:

- The consciousness of the water element works by diluting the mineral layers, thus splitting the lithosphere into minute particles. By whirling the particles around, a multitude of ever-changing constellations come into being, which act as models for the forthcoming forms of reality. In this phase, representing a synergy between the elements of water and earth, minerals appear diluted like ocean water.
- Following Gaia's forefinger (water element), the middle finger comes into action, and with it, consciousness of the fire element. I can see countless lines of fiery vital forces dancing around water-shaped primary forms of future bodies, while also penetrating them. The forms of the future reality come alive and start to breath.
- The last to enter the process is the little finger of Gaia's creative hand, and with it the aspect of consciousness. The consciousness of the air element uses patterns or codes as guidelines along which bodies and objects get their final form.

Since past and future are non-existent, mental categories, the creation process is not done once, but is forever repeated in each moment—certainly in each moment with slightly changed consequences. The body of matter is being renewed and changed in each successive moment. Particles of matter are constantly entering the constellations of the manifested world and leaving them again, returning into the inner layers of the lithosphere.

The process of manifesting the material face of reality is, in a mysterious way, "pressed" into each single moment. Yet it is mysterious only to the rational mind, which is extremely slow in its perceptions and cannot imagine that different sequences of the creation process appear simultaneously.

There is one more fantastic capacity of minerals that I would like to mention. Their memory is so wide that it is capable of holding the information and the living presence of complete worlds, holding them compressed within the mineral layers in a "nano" (minute) form.

As a result, the physical body of the human being, for example, appears as a relatively simple organism, but in effect, the entire vast universe is compressed within its mineral structures, and even much more. Looking at the physical body from outside, all the dimensions presented in this book seem non-existent, perhaps nothing but the outburst of an exaggerated artistic imagination. And yet they can be called forth from the mineral layers of the body with the help of corresponding keys or codes. I believe that the Gaia Touch body exercises are one of possible collections of such codes.

## A dangerous human intervention

Knowing the kind of dynamics that moves Gaia's creative hand, it is obvious that the role of her thumb—representing the fifth element—is missing in the description of the process through which materialized reality comes into being. It is clear that the four fingers are not capable of manifesting reality in its perfect form if the thumb is not collaborating. There must be a blockage that does not allow all the aspects of Gaia's creation that belong to the embodied world according to their nature to find their proper way to manifest. The elemental beings representing the active aspect of Gaia's thumb are being prevented from fulfilling their task in a perfect way. Why is this so?

The answer came in April of 2014. I had a dream during the time my wife, Marika, and I were carving for a lithopuncture project for the town Morro do Pilar in Brazil:

*Looking around I realize that everything—each grass blade, tree, animal, landscape, and phenomena of the human world—is cov-*

*ered with a thin transparent folio. The folio is lifted for a few moments away from the manifested world, and I can't believe my eyes! Turning around, everything I see is alive: rocks, buildings, plants… They are not moving around, but are glowing from inside. It is obvious that not only their material bodies are present, but also the causal dimensions that otherwise are hidden behind their forms.*

My interpretation is that human beings are misusing their position upon Gaia's creative hand. The misuse is in the role of the little finger, and with it, our capacity to act relatively autonomously in the realm of the planetary consciousness. We are adjusting manifested reality to the severe criteria of our rational mind. Anything that has no form in matter or does not imprint in the logical layer of our mind is being treated as non-existent. Misusing its position, the human mind is succeeding in spreading this folio over all of creation. This prevents the phenomena of the embodied world from displaying the whole spectrum of their existence. Particularly affected are the causal dimensions behind the manifested world.

Yet we are not dealing here with some kind of a magic act performed in a distant past, but with the human practice of the present. Each one of us contributes to the renewal of the invisible folio each time we look around with our eyes trained only on the material. The knowledge of selectively looking at the world around us is being taught from generation to generation. Family education imprints it into the memory of small children; and school education offers a systematic approach to this sinister practice of our minds. The dressing of the world with this fatal folio is strengthened with each new generation.

My proposal is to contribute to the liberation of the manifested world from this kind of human projection by following, from time to time, this Gaia Touch exercise:

PERSONAL RITUAL TO SUPPORT THE LIBERATION OF THE
MANIFESTED WORLD FROM THE SUPPRESSING HUMAN
PROJECTIONS

1. You can perform this ritual in a natural or an urban setting,
   in your home or in a garden.

2. Position one hand upright in front of your chest with the
   palm directed to the side. The tips of the fingers connect to
   the cosmic realms ("the upper worlds"). Hold the other hand
   pointing downward in front of your lower body, the palm
   directed to the side. Connect to the earthly realms with this
   hand ("the underworld").

3. While keeping the one hand up and the other down, imagine
   that you are holding a fine veil, a membrane, of rainbow
   colors between your hands. It is so large that it reaches to
   the edge of the horizon in form of a wide arch. The veil does
   not only touch the space above the Earth's surface, but also
   enters into the Earth. Thus the veil is circular; one half rising
   high over the ground, the other reaching deep into the Earth.

4. In this process, it is important, that the perimeter of the veil
   is not only carried by the hands, but also by the edge of your
   heart area. That is because the heart knows the touch of eternity and, by this, the truth of that very instant.

5. Now start moving with extreme care slowly to the right. Take
   the rainbow-colored veil along so that the ambience over and
   under the ground has to go through the veil. Take advantage
   of your imagination to make sure that indeed every inch of
   the ambience glides through the veil as you keep turning.

6. The ritual is finished, when the rainbow-veil has been led
   through a circle of 360°. It is good to repeat the exercise in
   the opposite direction.

## Minerals are at the core of human creation

By suppressing objects and beings of the materialized world, human consciousness is in an obvious contradiction of denying the very nature and makeup of ourselves and our world. The important role of the lithosphere relates to all the different forms and epochs of human culture, including our contemporary high-tech civilization. Minerals have played a decisive role in human culture from the use of stone tools in the Paleolithic age, across the history of building in stone and wood, to modern skyscrapers and motorways of steel, concrete, and glass. Even computers, our "artificial intelligence," would not work without the input of tiny pieces of the mineral silica.

The problem might be with human superstition—a self-conceived superiority. Not acknowledging the beings of the other four fingers as collaborating intelligences, we impose the illusion upon ourselves that we are sole the creators. Consequently, instead of walking the path of co-creation and co-existence with our partners in evolution, we independently develop methods and technologies that harm the natural order of the Earthly Cosmos and even poison its very base.

While pondering a work of art, be it a painting, a sculpture, or architecture; while walking the avenues of grand cities; or sitting behind a computer, we should be aware that it is all composed of microscopic particles of minerals, and feel gratitude toward all the beings of Gaia's hand for their help in creating the materialized reality of each new moment.

To conclude the first part of our journey I wish to propose a Gaia Touch group exercise meant to express reverence and gratitude to all the beings and worlds of the Earthly Cosmos.

## Group ritual to honor all beings and worlds of the Earthly Cosmos

1. The group is standing in a circle. Hold hands in a way that the thumbs are pointing to the right side, so the right hand receives and the left hand passes on. The energy moves in a clockwise direction. (This can be done also in the opposite direction.)

2. The group bends forward and deeply downward, with their hands pointing toward the Earth's center. In this way, we honor the worlds and beings inhabiting the Earth.

3. The group slowly straightens up and moves their hands high up to the sky, still holding hands, and bending backward as far as possible. By this, we honor the celestial level of the Earthly Cosmos.

4. Again bend forward and deeply downward. Repeat the movements several times. The arms should always be stretched out, also when lifting and lowering the hands.

5. At the end, the group stays still, standing in a circle for a while with the hands released in order to experience the moment.

# INTERMEZZO 1

Dear friend, I am happy you have accompanied me through the book up to this point of crossing, to this first Intermezzo. We have just concluded our walk along the horizontal arm of the cosmic cross. To remind you, it is the archetype of the cosmic cross that we use to orient ourselves on our journey through the universe of the human body.

Why identify some sections as "Intermezzo"? The word is Italian for "something in between." Its purpose here is to make a pause upon the path through the extensions of the integral human body, looking back at the path already left behind, and to ponder the plans for the future journey.

So, before we start to travel along the vertical arm of our key archetype, we should for a moment look at what has already been completed from the prospective of the great changes brought forward by the Earth transmutation process, as mentioned in the Prologue. A whole set of changes is waiting at the door of human consciousness. Waiting to be invited in to work on attuning human existence to the renewed body of the Earth.

## Human beings are leaning heavily upon animals

Let me start with the changes concerning the relationship between human beings and their animal ancestral line. As a consequence of human ignorance toward the animal-related roots of our existence on Earth, billions of animals are frozen within the bodies of the human species. Chained within the human subconscious realms, they are deprived of the possibility of taking part in the further development of their species.

Also, the gift of instinctive perception that we inherit from animals needs to be developed toward intuition. Such intuition is urgently needed at this time for individuals to maintain proper orientation in the whirlpool of global change. Instead, the primeval instinct inherited from the animals is largely distorted by the human species into innumerable expressions of fear. We need to face the truth of the changes coming upon the Earth, instead of fearing them. These are inevitable, fundamental changes to allow life a chance to continue.

I hear a clear call issued by innumerable animals worldwide, addressed to us humans. They are asking for us to give freedom to the animal within, so that it can follow the path of transformation that the animal species need to undergo during the present times of change. To be able to follow the winding path of change, our personal animal consciousness needs to re-connect with its archetype stored in the causal body "far behind our back."

I can see the treasury of animal archetypes stored in Earth's memory in the form of a paradise-like landscape immersed deeply into the realms of the causal world. It is the home of mythical animals, such as the unicorn or griffin. In the background of the manifested world, they represent the ancestors of the present-day animal species. We are dealing here with the causal dimension of the animal world that can be understood as the earthly complement to the cosmic zodiac.

Renewing the link of our inner animal with its archetype means that the potentials of its instinctive consciousness are awakened. Instinct is a gift of the animals that enables the human being to be connected to the laws of life. Living in an instinctive consciousness helps us not to lose the thread while following the impulses of our own matrix. This connects us to the essence of life, holding upright our will to be and our will to be true.

## New proportions between extensions of the human being

There are even more challenges facing the human race. The egocentric personality of the human being, for example, occupies the space allotted to the human identity. This problem was pinpointed in Chapter 7. Another challenge is our banishing of the personal elemental being from human awareness.

These problems can find their solution by radical changes in the proportions between the animal and elemental aspects of the human individuality. The role of personality and one's the relationship to one's soul must also shift. The changed proportions reflect basic shifts occurring in the constitution of the Earthly Cosmos as a result of the Earth Changes addressed in the Prologue.

The personal animal aspect should be allowed to reach backward into the realms of the causal world to re-connect with its archetype. The focus of personality should renounce its dominance over the human identity and find its new role in front of the body as a communicator between our individuality and the social and natural environment. The personal elemental being should be invited to become present in the human consciousness, moving closer to our essence. The individual soul should be allowed to permeate the whole human being with its wisdom. Instead of "floating above," it should become grounded in the human body, reaching all the way down to its soles.

On the following page is a Gaia Touch exercise to work on the described shifts in proportions.

## We climb along the vertical world axis

In the last chapters we passed through the three layers of the causal world (symbolically positioned behind the back) and the layers of the manifested world in front of the body. In the next chapters, we will change the direction of our journey through the spaces of the integral human body. We will shift from the horizontal axis of the cosmic cross, to the vertical. Traditionally, the vertical axis is called the *"axis mundi"* which is Latin for "axis of the world."

The vertical world axis represents the axis around which the tissue of the Earthly Cosmos is being constantly woven in collaboration with the wider holon of the cosmic dimensions and their beings. We shall begin at the bottom of the world axis associated with the Earth Soul. In the Prologue we got to know her as Gaia, the creator of life and its beings.

From there, we shall climb the world axis upward, following different phases of Gaia's creative process. We will get to know the majestic primeval powers of Gaia, known in mythical language as dragons. Our vertical climb will bring us to the level of the horizontal arm of the cosmic cross that we traveled along during the first part of the book. There the whole spectrum of living

GAIA TOUCH EXERCISE
TO EMBODY NEW PROPORTIONS
BETWEEN DIFFERENT ASPECTS
OF THE HUMAN BEING

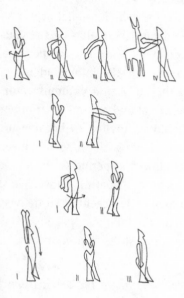

1. Join your hands at the heart level to connect with your personal inner animal. Imagine embracing your personal animal.

2. Since the personal animal is retreating toward your causal background, without turning around, imagine that it takes three steps backward. It stays there. Make the corresponding gesture with your hands as shown in the drawing.

3. Then return with your hands to your body and imagine grasping your personality and transferring it one step forward out of your body.

4. Through the movement of the personal animal and the personality out of your center, free space comes into being there. Take a moment to feel the changed quality within you.

5. The personal elemental being is the first to occupy the free space in your being. It had been working with your body from the causal level. Now it has more space in your personal noosphere to remind you of your birthright to exist as a being of the Earth. Reach with a corresponding gesture and bring it from your back space into the middle of your body space.

6. The second entity to occupy the free space at the center of your being is your soul, the carrier of your identity, which is pulsating beyond space and time. It should not float above the body any more. First bring it with a corresponding gesture down to the level of the heart. Continuing the gesture, you should then anchor it in the Earth below your feet.

7. Perform the gestures lovingly, yet with most possible precision, so that the beings involved can read them as instructions on how to follow the rhythms of change.

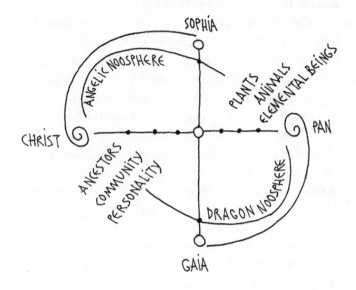

*The horizontal axis of life and the vertical axis of creation*

beings abiding at the Earth's surface is arranged, from elemental beings, animals, and plants to human beings, and including our cultural creations.

At this point we will jump to the highest point of the world axis, to the center of the universe, symbolically speaking, the center of our galaxy. From there we will descend toward the surface of the Earth to complete our traversing of the vertical axis of the cosmic cross.

## The key importance of the Earth's noosphere

Until now we have moved through the regions of human existence related more or less to the touchable faces of the Earthly Cosmos: animals, plants, human culture, etc. From now on, as we climb along the world axis, the conditions change. The levels positioned along the vertical axis have almost no fixed reference points. Are we condemned to stagger upon abstract esoteric fields?

I am convinced that in approaching the world axis we do not have to surrender to a spirituality alienated from the reality of life.

The concept of the touchable world as the only existing reality is an illusion of the alienated human mind. Ignoring or denigrating these worlds is an excuse to avoid the more complex levels of reality that are foreign to the rational mind, as well as an excuse to avoid learning the language to communicate with them.

From a holistic point of view, living reality is a result of mutual interaction between the five fingers of Gaia's creative hand, as discussed in Chapter 2. Usually the world operates through the interaction of the five elements in collaboration with the palm of Gaia's hand. Here is a short description:

- Gaia's palm stands for the matrix of the Earthly Cosmos being constantly woven at the core of the planet.
- The thumb of Gaia's creative hand symbolizes the activity of all beings working as mediators, translating the matrix of the Earthly Cosmos into different processes through which the manifested world comes into existence.
- The forefinger of Gaia's creative hand stands for the water element and the interflow of vital powers — called also "bio-energy."
- The middle finger stands for the fire element and the inspirations igniting creative processes upon the Earth.
- The ring finger stands for the earth element and the capacity of Gaia to bring about different forms of embodiment, be it in dense or subtle matter.
- Gaia's small finger marks the air element, standing for the planetary consciousness sphere, shared by all beings of the Earth when thinking, imagining, or feeling.

Each phenomenon on the Earth's surface represents a specific combination of the above listed aspects of Gaia's creative hand.

In the case of the "middle world," visited while walking upon the horizontal arm of the cosmic cross, the forms of embodiment play the dominant role. The focus changes along the vertical world axis. These mainly express through different levels of consciousness.

We need to be aware, step after step, that reality is first of all an expression of consciousness. The sphere of consciousness, the so-called noosphere, is a sphere shared by all worlds and beings of the Earth and universe. It is inwardly richly structured and

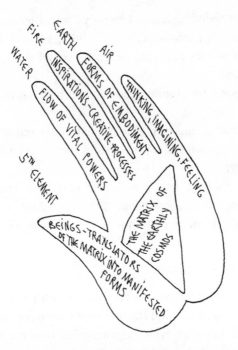

*Gaia's creative hand at the consciousness level*

works in an integrating way. Understanding different facets of the noosphere has nothing to do with ungrounded spirituality. Even when moving through realms where there is no trace of matter or energy, we should be resolute about the conviction that we are moving upon a ground not less real then the materialized world, just different.

## Take care, dangerous realms!

Climbing upon the world axis, we shall inevitably come in contact with some aspects of existence that, unfortunately, are dividing people today, sometimes in a rather terrible way. I refer to those realms that bear religious association. Yet we cannot avoid them and are not allowed to do so if we wish to experience the totality of the human universe and be equitable toward all realms of the universal whole.

There are religious people to whom the sacred dimensions of nature and the Earth seem a sacrilege in the face of God. On the other side are individuals standing only for limitless human autonomy, denying any relationship to divinity, such as the scientific view, which refuses to speak about the sacred dimensions of the material world.

My proposal for reconciliation between opposing views is as follows:

- Try to find a language that is neutral, as much as possible, so that the realms along the world axis will be accessible to everybody.

- Present this book as a piece of artwork. This creates a space secure enough to allow people to change their standpoint and renounce certain preconceptions—if this is needed.

### Geocentric or heliocentric?

There is one more theme that can lead to conflict if not clarified in advance. I have in mind the opposition between the geocentric model of the universe, which is focused at the core of the Earth, and the model focused at the core of the Sun, known as "heliocentric," after Helios, the Greek god of the Sun.

Walking the horizontal path of Gaia's worlds, we moved constantly within the orbit of the Earth. The Sun assumed a side role, as in the case of the plants. It was natural to feel the Earth, in this case, as the center of the universe. From now on the situation will change. We will find ourselves in the energy field of two equal centers. On one side, the position of Gaia at the core of her universe should not be denied. On the other hand, we will get to know, in the figure of Sophia, the other center of the universe—embodied by our home star, the Sun.

Seen from the point of view of Gaia, the whole universe is turning around her core—the Sun, the planets, and distant star systems included. Seen from the prospective of the Sun, the situation is turned inside out. The Earth together with its complete (micro-) universe is one of the spheres of Sophia's creation that is dancing around the Sun. The geo- and heliocentric systems are both right and needed.

The polarization between the two systems finds its final solution if the third player in the cosmic game gets her needed attention—

the Moon. The Moon, which I prefer to call by the Latin name "Luna," is the sister of Gaia and is responsible for the planet's water body, moving its oceans in the rhythm of ebb and flow. In another aspect, she reflects the solar light in a cyclical way. She is the neutral link between the Earth and the Sun. She is the Queen of the Night.

# PART 11

# THE VERTICAL PATH

# 1

# THE GAIA-CENTERED EARTHLY COSMOS

This chapter is dedicated to Gaia, the Mother of Life, flourishing within the Earthly Cosmos. Now we start, dear co-traveler, to explore the vertical axis of our orientation chart, which has the form of the cosmic cross. As promised, we shall begin our path at the deepest point of the world axis, the Earth's core. To be able to approach safely the core of the planet, brilliant as a star, we shall help ourselves with some wisdom from the ancient myths and traditions. Mythos offers a buffer, which is needed to avoid possible shock in approaching the tremendous power of Gaia.

## A Slovenian Gaia mythos

The mythos of the fish Faronika is preserved in a Slovenian folk poem dating from very ancient times. Its ancient origin is seemingly contradicted by Jesus being mentioned in the first line. But this was clearly added at a later date to preserve the precious oral tradition from being destroyed in the age under Christian dominance. The mythology of a fish carrying the world on its back is known also to some other cultures, like the Tibetan one. The name "Faronika" ("the one of the pharaoh") in Slovenian tradition probably comes from the biblical story of the army of the Egyptian pharaoh drowned in the Red Sea while pursuing the Jews on their flight to Sinai. In the folklore imagination, the soldiers were transformed into undersea monsters with a human body and a double fish tail.

*Jesus is swimming in the sea, in a deep sea.*
*A fish woman is following him, it is Faronika.*
*"O wait fish woman, wait fish woman Faronika!*
*I want to ask you what is happening in the world."*

*"If I flip my tail then the world will be flooded.*
*If I turn onto my back then the world will perish."*

*The fish woman Faronika from a medieval fresco in Slovenia*

*"O don't do it fish woman, fish woman Faronika.*
*Think of the little children, don't do it,*
*And think of all women in childbirth."*

The fish is a relevant symbol for Gaia, the Earth Soul. Fish live in the great depths of the sea, similar to the Earth Soul, which has its abode at the center of the Earthly Cosmos. Fish are mute, and yet the eyes speak of a consciousness that is beyond human imagination. The idea that the condition of our world at the surface depends on the movements set in motion by the Earth Soul is also typically associated with Gaia. And Gaia is clearly designated as a feminine goddess, as is the being of the fish in the poem. In my country, there are frescoes from the Middle Ages that show her as a naked woman with a double tail and a crown.

This Slovenian folk poem conveys an image of the manifested world as a disc floating upon the deep sea of the causal world. In the first chapter we called it "the liquid universe," which means a world stratum where forms are not yet defined. Only the relevant patterns of their existence are vibrating beyond space and time determination.

Further it needs to be emphasized that the fish is floating in the liquid universe of the deep sea. Today we know that sea water is as rich with the life-giving substances as the "fruit water" from the womb. Indeed, in the last line of the poem "all women in childbirth" is mentioned to point out that Gaia can be understood as a large, planet-embracing womb, i.e., the primeval source of life's abundance. Yet the Earth Soul is not just a source of life, but also a vast consciousness capable of communication—a characteristic of Gaia revealed in the poem through the dialogue with Jesus.

## The Grail mythos addresses the threefold gift of Gaia

The Grail mythos is another traditional source containing essential knowledge about the essence of Gaia, the Earth Soul. As in the case of the folk poem about Faronika, the roots of the Grail mythos can be traced far back into human history. Its form is known from the Middle Ages. Among different versions of the Grail mythos, I trust the one written by the German poet Wolfram von Eschenbach between the 12th and 13th centuries as the Parzival epos. From von Eschenbach I have learned to know three basic qualities of the Holy Grail that represent a relevant imagination of who Gaia is and her role in the Earthly Cosmos. They can be found in Chapter 10 of the epos, when Parzival's hermit uncle (Trevrizent) explains to him the meaning of the Grail symbols. Let me translate them from mythic images into the language of logic:

- Gaia, being identical with the Holy Grail, is the source of the Earth's fertility. Translated: This symbolizes Gaia, the Earth Soul, as capable of developing our home planet to exist as a living organism. Through the work of her elemental worlds, Gaia is upholding and renewing the Earth's fertility at each moment anew.

- Gaia, being identical with the Holy Grail, is the source of life's abundance. Translated: Gaia is the primeval cause behind the evolutionary process through which the complete spectrum of life forms and beings, visible and invisible, develop and expand upon the Earth, including those materialized in the form of minerals, plants, animals, and humans.

- Gaia, being identical with the Holy Grail, is the source of poetic inspirations. Translated: This means something revolutionary—Gaia is not just the moving principle behind the life processes, but also a consciousness that is capable of inspiring creative processes, i.e., to introduce changes that are beyond evolutionary logic. Especially, her role is emphasized as the source of artistic inspiration.

Besides these three basic qualities of Gaia, Trevrizent tells Parzival about three further dimensions of the Earth Soul:

- Gaia, in the role of the Holy Grail, is symbolized by a black stone called "lapis exilis." Through the stone symbol, we get to know the miraculous tool that Gaia uses to manifest her creations upon the Earth's surface. I have in mind the richly structured world of minerals. Collaborating with the mineral kingdom, Gaia is capable of giving to each phenomena of life a proper body, be it in subtle or denser form.
- Trevrizent's words that the stone loses its creative power if not renewed yearly by the touch of the "turtledove of the Holy Spirit," refers to the vertical axis of the Earthly Cosmos that we are about to explore. As mentioned earlier in the chapter, the cosmic complement of Gaia is known as Sophia, the Wisdom of Eternity. Trevrizent's words mean that the creative power of Gaia is renewed through her interaction with the cosmic realms, symbolized by Sophia.
- The Grail mythos confirms Gaia as the all-embracing consciousness of the Earth. Trevrizent explains to Parzival that the names of those who are called to the Holy Grail appear in luminous letters on the surface of the Grail stone. This means that with the help of her noosphere, Gaia entertains a personal relationship with each being evolving within its Earthly universe, potentially also with each member of the human race.

For one's own experiences of the three qualities of Gaia in the context of the Grail mythos, I can propose the following Gaia Touch exercise:

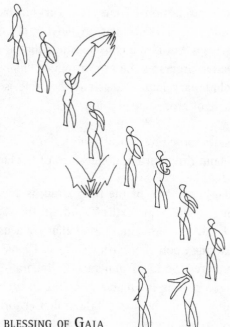

THE THREEFOLD BLESSING OF GAIA

1. Join your hands at the back of your coccyx in a "V" form similar to a plant root. The tips of the four fingers, representing the four elements, touch each other (the thumbs come into play later). Rest like this for a while, enjoying the connection with Gaia as the source of life.

2. Move your hands forward to the front of your belly, forming a large horizontal circle. In effect you have brought forward a vessel containing Gaia's fruits of life, which she donates to all beings of the manifested world. You may repeat the gesture three times, and then ponder for a while the created "Gaia's horn of abundance."

3. Next ask for the blessing of the cosmic aspect of Gaia (Sophia) by lifting your hands up with a pointing gesture. The inner sides of the hands are facing each other. This time all five finger tips are touching each other, while the palms are apart. (The thumbs represent the fifth element.)

4. Bring the blessing down into the vessel with the help of another pointing gesture—this time the back sides of the hands are facing each other. Bring it down beyond your solar plexus. Then the Grail vessel should be created again by forming the large horizontal circle again.

5. Repeat the set of gestures three times. Three times for the three qualities of the Holy Grail.

6. Accentuate the third quality of the Holy Grail, Gaia's creative inspiration, with the third iteration.

7. Bring your hands to the center of your heart space using a pointing gesture (the back sides of the hands face each other) and lead the blessing of your heart into the vessel with an opening gesture. Afterward, the circle of the Grail vessel should be created anew to make clear the source of inspiration.

8. Repeat the connection between your heart and the source of inspiration three times.

9. Finally, open the vessel by opening your hands horizontally as far into your back space as possible. While opening the circle, go backward with your head to open your whole body. Let the threefold blessing of Gaia be distributed across the world.

## The Grail mythos warns us not to abandon our relationship with the Earth Soul

Another set of messages conveyed by the Grail mythos should not be overlooked. They show the Grail family in distress. Amfortas, the Grail King, is irreparably wounded in his genitals. Put into logical, rather than imaginative terms, this says that our sacred relationship to Gaia, as celebrated since Neolithic times, no longer has a future. The patriarchal age brought to the human race a destructive will to abandon its intimate relationship with the Earth Soul. This disconnect from the Earth Soul caused an unhealthy pattern to develop. Human individuals have become autonomous beings, leaning too heavily upon only logical ways of thinking and making decisions.

Throughout millennia the human race worshiped Gaia under many diverse names, mostly as our Mother Earth. She was continuously venerated through ritual, color, dance, etc., and some aboriginal tribes today still worship her in this way. By continuous worshiping throughout millennia, human cultures upheld the bridge between the causal worlds of Gaia and her manifested creation. This is mostly gone now. What does the growing separation between Gaia and the human race mean?

Each of the five kingdoms has a different role to play in the dance of life upon the Earth's surface. Similar to the contributions of the animals, plants, minerals, and elemental beings, the human race needs to add its specific contribution to the "technology" for translating the creative vibrations of Gaia Consciousness (the Grail impulses) into living and touchable reality. But if one of the five fingers of Gaia's creative hand fails to perform its role, then the whole building of the manifested world is in danger of crumbling.

The present patriarchal age has caused this exact situation. The creative relationship with the Earth Soul is not just neglected by the human race but has also been perverted, be it through destruction of her living spaces or through robbing her treasures. What can be done to divert the path from self-destruction to a path of conscious cooperation with Gaia's creative potentials?

To offer a possible solution, the Grail mythos foresees the appearance of a new generation of Gaia's devotees, symbolized by Parzival, the Grail seeker. The intuition of the mythos, translated into the language of logic, can be expressed in three points:

- Human beings have to decide individually whether to follow the illusions and projections generated by the one-sidedness of the present civilization, or to go forward and search ceaselessly for one's true essence in relation to Gaia, the creatress of the Earthly Cosmos.

- Humanity needs to become aware that enjoying creative freedom on Earth demands also accepting co-responsibility for the well-being of all the other creatures, visible and invisible, with whom we share Gaia's house.

- A tolerant, loving and co-creative relationship between the feminine and masculine principle within each of us is the indispensable precondition to existing as a human family in peace and mutual respect, sharing the creative fruits of our community with other beings.

## Gaia as a potent Creatress

Seen from the point of view of the logical mind, Gaia's creative process presently exists in a frozen state. One cannot imagine that the exquisite beauty of butterflies and flowers could be optimized. Could the wonderful diversity of the Earth's landscapes be optimized? Human laboratories produce genetically modified plants, seemingly adding to nature's diversity. However, many of us believe that rather than a victorious post-evolution of Gaia's creation the results are in new forms of allergies.

My following dream may help in understanding where Gaia's creative potentials are at work now:

*The train stands still on the track. There is no engine to pull us forward. We passengers are tired of waiting for a possible solution. We do not believe we will move forward ever again. Then the news starts to circle among us that an express train is arriving with great speed upon the same track. Are we facing a deadly disaster?*

My interpretation is that the train standing still on the track without the engine to pull it forward represents the present situation upon the Earth. We are prisoners of a creation that is frozen by the exclusive concepts of human rationality. In effect, all levels of the Earth's creative process are ignored, except those manifested in physical form or perceived through the eyes of logic. The abundance of Gaia's universe is being compressed into one single flat plane.

*Finally the feared express train arrives. Without causing any harm, it glides in the form of a train of light through our dense train.*

The dream brought awareness that even if seemingly blocked at present time, Gaia's creative process continues. In the present epoch, her creative potentials are obviously moving upon another level of reality. This higher reality is symbolized by the high-speed train. Still attached to the rational way of perceiving reality, human culture is presently unable to recognize the continuation of Gaia's creative process. We stay connected to our limited perceptions with the same intensity as in the past; however, another level of reality enfolds us.

In the Prologue I have presented my experiences of the present Earth Changes as a process of transmutation, including my perception of where it leads. By calling it a "transmutation process," I intend to emphasize that we are not dealing with a linear succession of changes, but with a process affecting the very constitution of the reality in which we abide. Gaia, as a mighty Creatress, is creating a new space and time structure underlying our reality, allowing presently invisible aspects of the multidimensional body of reality to manifest in a less or more dense form.

This is "the high-speed train" of Gaia's creation. For 15 years I have observed fundamental changes in the body of the Earth and its noosphere in rhythmical succession and with amazing speed. Is this not a sign that Gaia is fully active as a creating agent?

### The pattern of Gaia as Mother Earth is out of date

To be able to understand Gaia's present-day creative input we need to free her from the "Mother Earth" pattern, as far as it binds her exclusively to the role of moving life streams upon the planet. This is only one of her roles. Complementing it, Gaia should be recognized as a cosmic intelligence, a *maestra* of creation, taking part in a creative process that touches the universe as a whole. Her creative workshop should not be searched anywhere but upon the Earth and among us, its beings, but the resonance of her work might be felt throughout the universe.

To enable the transformation of the outdated pattern, it is of decisive importance to become aware of Gaia's interaction with Sophia (touched upon in connection with the Grail mythos). In the universal process of creation, they collaborate like two faces of one and the same being, one existing at the level of the planet and the other throughout the widths of the universe.

The following Gaia Touch exercise is meant to give us an intimate experience of Gaia as a universal Creatress capable of weaving the cosmic inspiration of Sophia into her own creative process. The exercise starts with Gaia's creative powers emanating from the

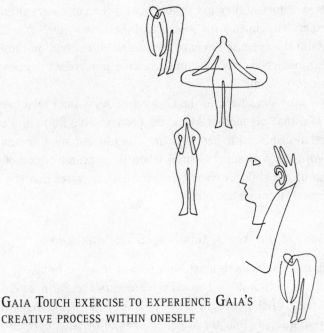

## GAIA TOUCH EXERCISE TO EXPERIENCE GAIA'S CREATIVE PROCESS WITHIN ONESELF

1. Bow down toward the inner Earth where Gaia is maintaining the archetypal powers of water that are basic in the creation of life. Form a small pot with your hands and scoop with it the water of the primeval powers. Bring it up to the level of your solar plexus.

2. Distribute its quality in the form of a blue watery field around you, reaching to the fringe of your energy field. Take some time to experience how it feels to be involved in the creative process of Gaia.

3. Lift your hands so they meet at the root of the nose. Be aware that through this gesture you add your creative intelligence to the process. Make a short pause to affirm your presence in the process.

4. Move slowly with your hands in a horizontal direction toward your ears, all the time touching the skull. After reaching the place behind your auricles, stay there and embrace them with your hands. Push the ears a bit forward as if indicating you are listening to the cosmic inspiration.

5. Afterward, bend toward the inner Earth again. Repeat the exercise at least two times more.

core of the Earth and surfacing through the medium of water. In the next sequence they get in touch with the cosmic inspiration, the aspect associated with Sophia and the cosmic intelligence. At this point the exercise refers to the so-called "conception through the ear" which means initiating creative processes by receiving cosmic inspiration.

The story goes back to the Gospels of Jesus the Christ, where it is said that his mother Mary did not conceive through a sexual relationship with her husband Joseph, but by listening to the words of Archangel Gabriel when he appeared to announce arrival of her child. A corresponding myth narrates that she has conceived "through her ears."

## The body of the oceans, Gaia's vehicle of expression

Without a doubt there must be a reason that the folk song featuring the fish woman Faronika represents the Earth soul as a giant fish. A fish resides in water. A giant fish lives in the oceans. The resolution is that the water masses of oceans represent the medium through which Gaia is present upon the Earth surface— to put it exactly, the oceans facilitate direct contact between the Earth Soul and the planet's biosphere.

The most important relationship is between the Pacific and Atlantic oceans. Their gigantic water masses are positioned on either side of Earth's globe, thus being responsible for the planet's equilibrium and contributing to the development of the biosphere at its surface.

To be able to hold balance, emphasized in the Fish Faronika myth as one of Gaia's priorities, both oceans need to be polarized regarding their role in the planetary water body. The Portuguese explorer Ferdinand Magellan, who was the first to cross the Pacific, gave it the name "Ocean of Peace" because he was astonished by its peaceful nature. The name is not without reason. It relates to the role of the Pacific Ocean within the Earth's water body. The mineral substance of the ocean's water receives information from the vastness of the universe, holding it in its memory to enrich the archetypes of life emerging constantly from the core of Gaia. The focus of the Pacific Ocean is turned outside-in.

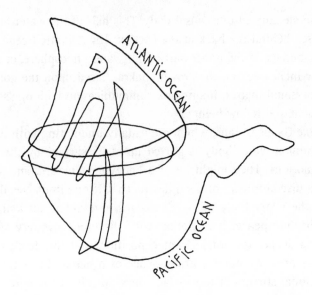

*The Atlantic and Pacific oceans related to the human body*

The name of the Atlantic Ocean is associated with the ancient civilization of Atlantis, which was considered to be a watery civilization. The idea of a civilization can be understood as a symbol for the more active role of the Atlantic, turned inside-out toward communication. The Atlantic appears to my perception as a vast noosphere extending over the adjacent continents and high into the atmosphere. The noosphere of the Atlantic relates to the manifested world of nature and culture. Receiving impulses from the core of the Earth, it distributes the creative ideas of Gaia among the landscapes and beings of the planet.

## Gaia's oceans and the human water body

When speaking about the human water body, we should think of a rounded-up egg-like sphere of water consciousness surrounding the human figure and permeating it. As in the case of the Earth's macrocosm, the noosphere of the human water body is polarized.

The lower part, under the diaphragm, resonates with the Pacific Ocean in that it connects the human being with its matrix, stored in the memory of our causal body. This half of the water body is focused behind the back at the coccyx. The Atlantic Ocean finds its resonance in the upper part of our watery noosphere, centered a few inches behind the crown chakra. Based upon the codes of our personal matrix, it supports communication with one's environment and fellow beings.

Like Gaia's oceans, which are usually undulating with waves, the human water body is stirred up at its surface by the wind of emotions. They might be of a benevolent nature, and sometimes discomforting or even destructive. If one immerses deeper into the water body of Gaia's oceans, one enters an ambience of absolute peace. It is similar with the human watery sphere. Diving deeper toward its center, positioned at the depth of the plexus area, we enter a grand space of peace and serenity. The emotional stirring at the surface does not affect the core of the human water body.

The two halves of the human water body touch and permeate each other in the realm between the pelvic cavity and the chest. Here is located the focus of the Earth's soul—of the Fish Faronika—within our body's watery sphere. Around this wonderful center of peace and serenity, the water masses of our fluid body are rotating in slow motion, rising along the back side of the body upward and following the front side downward.

A similar balancing system can be found between the Atlantic and Pacific oceans. While working in the cityscape of Quito, the capital of Ecuador, I perceived it in the form of two parallel light channels crossing Central America, one above Ecuador and the island of San Juan, Puerto Rico, and the other over the Yucatan and Florida. Their purpose is to balance the two oceans, allowing the flux of information in one or another direction as needed in a given moment to secure the planet's equilibrium.

It is nearly impossible to emphasize enough how important it is for our inner peace and for the peace of the world that the subtle movements of our water body are balanced and focused around this point of peace, identical with the focus of Gaia. If we succeed, then the vibration of our emotions can be easily attuned to the impulses of the heart, the backbone finds a secure support, and our intimate link to the Mother of life is secured.

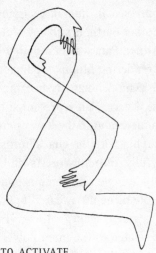

GAIA TOUCH EXERCISE TO ACTIVATE
THE PERSONAL WATER BODY

1. Touch with the fingers of one hand the place on your skull positioned three inches behind the crown chakra. Here you enter in resonance with the Atlantic Ocean and the corresponding sphere of your water body.

2. At the same time, go with the other hand to your back space to touch the back of the coccyx. Here you enter in resonance with the quality of the Pacific Ocean and the second half of your water body.

3. After a short while, exchange the positions of the two hands. Repeat exchanging the positions a few times.

4. Stop the movements and turn your attention to the point of perfect peace at the depth of your solar plexus. Enjoy this peace for a while.

5. Then go in your imagination from there to the bottom of the ocean. There you will find a door to go even a step deeper into the abode of the Earth Soul. Look into the eyes of the giant fish there, and bring its peace up to the space of your heart. Share it with the world around you.

## Pan as Gaia's masculine complement

We always celebrate Gaia's goddess aspect. Does she know a masculine complement? Is Gaia married to someone?

Indeed, Gaia has a partner but his presence is even more severely suppressed in human consciousness than hers is. Gaia, at least as Mother Earth, is still celebrated in some aboriginal cultures. Her partner, Pan, was humiliated in medieval Christianity to the point of rendering him as the image of the devil, a symbol of ultimate evil. Gaia deliberately became a widow!

In ancient Greece, Pan represented the God of Nature. He was depicted as a male goat in the lower part of his body, and above as a male human but with the goat's horns. As such he was supposed to move joyfully through forests and landscapes dancing with nymphs and playing on his famous pan flute. His image regressed later to the role of being a feared opponent of God, the devil. In effect, Pan became a scapegoat, carrying on his shoulders all the human fears related to the inner power of nature, of Gaia, and of the elemental kingdom—fears plaguing the human race because of its lost connection to its own inner nature.

Gaia representing the Earth Soul can be imagined as the inner sun of the Earth. Radiating with her creative powers from the core of the planet toward its surface, she initiates life processes upon the Earth, allowing all beings, human included, to share in her consciousness. Gaia is the Soul of the Earth and the source of its precious life.

Pan represents the Spirit of the Earth. Complementary to Gaia, he works from the opposite direction, from outside, taking care of all life forms evolving upon the planet's surface. His task is to hold them permanently connected to the core of the Earthly Cosmos. He is the keeper of Earth's identity, while Gaia is the Mother of our planetary life.

Entering the sphere of Pan's consciousness I feel connected to every cell in the body of nature, experiencing myself as present at the sacred center where all beings of nature are one. Furthermore, I learned from a series of experiences of Pan's two phases of existence:

- Pan represents the focal point through which all the beings and powers of nature belonging to a certain holon can relate to their matrix. In this phase, each place or landscape knows its own Pan and the place of his focus. From there Pan works as a

*Pan as the Celtic god Cernunos, perceived in a park in Türnich, Germany*

parabolic mirror, reflecting the code of their true selves toward all the beings of the given region.

- Pan can also be experienced as one integral noosphere omnipresent in nature's realms of the Earth's surface. As such, he can appear at any time, anywhere, if there is a reason and a nature-loving atmosphere.

To be fair to the relationship between Pan and Gaia, I would eliminate the human-given epithet "married couple." I would rather speak of two complementary principles permeating the Earthly Cosmos, enabling the evolution of life on the planet to take the optimal course.

### The masculine principle manifested in the human body

As for the Earth so also for each of us, whether being woman or man, balance between the feminine and masculine principles is of great importance. In the case of the Earth, the balance is symbolized in the relationship between Gaia and Pan. Relating to the human being, we know that the feminine principle expresses through the binary nature of the water body. Is it not logical that the masculine principle would use the language of the fire element to express itself?

Envision a vertical line of five centers positioned along the vertical axis of the human body. I call this composition "the scepter of the masculine power." It needs to be emphasized that the scepter of power is not reserved to masculine individuals, but vibrates within each woman and each man as a precondition of the ability to use creative capacities. Also it should be stressed that the success of the scepter could be minimal or could easily collapse to become destructive if not used in cooperation with the feminine principle vibrating in our water body.

Here are the main characteristics of the five centers of the scepter of power and their approximate locations in the body. This can be understood as an alternative to the well-known alignment of the seven chakras that comes forward in the context of the present-day Earth changes.

- At the central point of the pelvic cavity, the center of the perfect presence is located. If present there, then one becomes at one with the whole Earthly Cosmos. In the first chapter of Part III we will give special attention to this point.
- The next center of the scepter of power can be found where the two halves of our water body interact, in the area of the solar plexus. This second center connects the human being with the parallel worlds located on the horizontal axis of the world, be it the causal ones behind our back or the manifested layers in front of the body, which makes it possible for the parallel worlds to be included in the human creative processes.
- The point of the scepter, located at the lower end of the breastbone, represents the human capability to translate inspiration issuing from the core of the Earth and the universe into manifested forms. This was mentioned already before as the elemental heart of the human being.
- At the level of the heart center, the complex identity of the human individual is anchored and continuously renewed. It works within the scepter of power as a holographic piece of divinity that moves the universe. The space of the human heart will be discussed in the Part III.

*Author's cosmogram dedicated to the balance between the feminine (the crown composed of water drops) and the masculine (the scepter) principles.*

- The center behind the root of the nose could be called "the fairy's eye." It is sensitive to the messages of the Earth and the universe that enable visions to be developed, representing the initial force to move creative processes toward their embodiment.

The scepter of the masculine power plays a decisive role when creative and vital movements are about to take form and to manifest in day-to-day reality. It needs to be emphasized again that it has zero power if it does not cooperate with the cycles of the feminine water body. Cooperation can be initiated at any of scepter's five centers through a kind of sacred marriage between the feminine and masculine aspects of our individual being. This yin/yang relationship eclipses the archaic dominance of the masculine pole in the creative processes.

The following Gaia Touch exercise shows how the two principles complement each other in a new way. The masculine powers that have dominated for millennia over the feminine principle are in the process of retreating from the role of the grand activist dominating manifested reality. They will be rooted again in the causal back space, representing a strong background to the feminine principle, moving the world forward in a wise and loving way. A final gesture integrates the masculine principle, positioned now at the back, into activities performed in the manifested world.

GAIA TOUCH EXERCISE TO
EMBODY THE NEW ROLE OF
THE FEMININE AND MASCULINE
PRINCIPLES WITHIN US

1. Position both hands at the
   side of your chest at the
   level of your heart to come
   into resonance with the
   masculine principle within
   you. Your fists are strongly
   clenched to indicate that
   you relate to the masculine
   powers of the heart. While
   the hands are clenched, the
   thumbs are not compressed
   but rest upon your fists.

2. Stay for a while in the
   sunshine of your heart to connect the masculine principle
   again with the power of the heart.

3. Reach with your hands outstretched into your back space
   to indicate the new position of the masculine principle connected now to your causal levels. The fists are still clenched!
   The backward movement ends behind your buttocks.

4. Release your fists and imagine gliding tenderly forward,
   along your belly space, with the palms outstretched. The gesture ends in front of the body as if holding a vessel or a grail.

5. Stay for a while like this to feel how it is when you act in the
   world in a feminine way while supported by the masculine
   aspect at your back.

6. Move with the open hands upward along the body, bringing
   the feminine quality up to the top and around the head.
   (This shows that the masculine aspect is integrated.) The
   movement ends with the hands open in the gesture of opening the joint feminine and masculine powers to the world.

7. Now you can start from the beginning, positioning both
   hands at the side of your chest...

8. Repeat the exercise for a while in a rhythmical manner, then
   stand still and listen to the quality that comes into being.

## 2
# ATOMIC POWER – DRAGON CONSCIOUSNESS

Upon entering the house of our integral body we should be aware that several of its rooms have been locked or even sealed for centuries or even millennia. Individuals have run into deadly danger if they dared to enter. As a result, the proper language to address different dimensions of the multidimensional body of the Earth or human being was lost. To be able to speak now about such phenomena, I am often forced to use a kind of a crazy combination of fairy tale imaginary and rational logic. This applies also to the realm of the primeval powers of the Earth traditionally associated with the world of dragons.

*Dragons represent the primeval powers of the Earth*

Dragons appear in the mythical traditions of many cultures worldwide as double-faced beings. They can bestow upon the human race all the fortune of the Earthly Cosmos or cause merciless destruction. As such, they symbolize the primeval powers of Earth and cosmos before they are polarized, ordered, and transformed into vital energy and the corresponding forms of consciousness. In the language of classical Greek philosophy they are called the forces of Chaos — Chaos as a precondition for the ordered cosmos to appear.

The chaotic nature of the primeval powers can best be imagined if compared with the fiery turbulences appearing on the surface of the Sun. They are so powerful that they illuminate our whole solar system, the Earth globe and its Moon included. How grateful we are for the daily light that we all enjoy! Yet there is also the destructive face of that light that we know from the devastating consequences of atomic bomb explosions, capable of extinguishing life in a split second.

The mythical image of dragons stands for the consciousness of the primeval powers of Gaia. Emitting primeval powers from her fiery core, Gaia enables a richly structured vital organism to

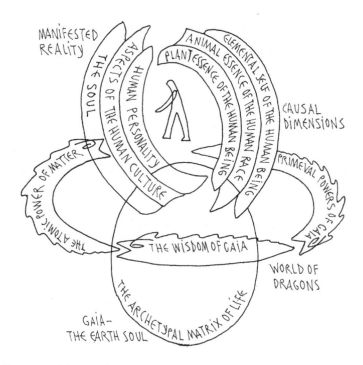

*The place of dragons in the relationship between Gaia and the human being*

appear upon the planet's surface in the form of a multitude of embodied, or even materialized, beings. This is possible because the primeval energy emanating from the star-like core of the Earth passes through different dimensions of Gaia's consciousness, and finally through the mineral layers of the Earth's shell, to be gradually transformed into life energy. It is the dragon power transformed into life energy that finally nourishes and sustains the landscapes and all of Gaia's beings living on the planet.

## A short history of dragons

Dragons represent the strange consciousness of the Earth's archetypal (primeval) powers. As such, they appear in different traditions as mystical animals such as dinosaur-like beings spitting fire out of their jaws. These images often emit a clear warning, trying to convey to the human race the message of how vulnerable we are in the face of the omnipotent powers of Gaia. Consequently, the early tribal cultures paid deep respect to the world of dragons.

This kind of relationship started to change at the threshold of the Iron Age, about three millennia ago, when cultures appeared that began to ignore the rules of life governing our home planet. The human race was about to break its bonds with the Mother of Life. To become more independent from her guidance, the Iron Age cultures developed myths and ritual practices to banish the all-prevailing power of Gaia's primeval forces. In this situation the mythos of the "dragon slayer" was invented, and heroes appeared such as the Germanic Siegfried, who was supposedly stronger then the primeval powers of the dragon and capable of subjugating them. In the Christian tradition the dragon world was distorted to the extent of becoming a symbol of evil that needs to be conquered. Saint George became the celebrated Christian version of the ancient dragon slayers. But do not believe that the awkward pattern of the dragon slayer is out of date! Not at all!

In our modern age the figure of the dragon slayer has been transformed into the dangerous practice of splitting or artificially fusing atoms to produce electricity, or to sow death among enemies. As a result, the devastating face of the dragon was awakened without awareness of the dragon's sacred role in the life-creating process.

The modern day manipulation of atomic power is directly opposing the wisdom of Gaia. In the epochs prior to our materialized world, the Mother of Life was capable of turning the power of the dragon outside-in, safely embedding it into the shell of the atom. In this way the destructive aspect of the primeval powers is allayed without suppressing its immense energy or humiliating its dragon consciousness. By "laying the dragon to sleep," Gaia has paved the way for subtle beings like plants, animals, humans, water, and minerals to embody in matter. We are able to walk around without heavy protective shields. Even though our bodies are composed of atomic structures, we are not burned out by the immense power of the dragon inherent within each atom constituting our materialized organism. We can happily enjoy life and develop our creativity.

### Dramatics of the "Atomic age"

Through modern manipulation of atomic power and the many atomic test explosions, the noosphere of the dragon force is gradually being awakened. The disaster with Japan's atomic plant at Fukushima is the ultimate sign of warning. Atomic manipulation is a direct counterforce to Gaia's effort to make the presence of primeval powers upon the Earth's surface safe by laying the ancient dragon to sleep within the atomic structures. As a consequence of the forceful awakening of the old dragon, all living beings are facing the danger of extinction—humanity included. This is a path of no return, as we all know.

And yet I believe that there is a way to avoid the possible suicide that would result from the misuse of atomic power. We need to face the challenge and cooperate with Gaia and other cosmic beings in the work of transforming the human projections that have pushed the dragon power into the role of destroyer, which is foreign to the dragon's true angelic quality of consciousness.

What do I mean by the dragon's angelic quality of consciousness?

Summarizing my geomantic experiences when working with the sacred places of the dragon, I dare to affirm that behind the ancient terrifying image of the dragon is hidden a consciousness sphere of angel-like beings. Of course, I do not imagine angels as winged puppets but as representatives of the noosphere of the universe. Dragons, standing for a specific aspect of Gaia's consciousness working within the Earthly Cosmos, are complementary to the angelic consciousness spread throughout the universe.

What is problematic is the dragon's forceful awakening through atomic manipulation. In such a case, the dragon's power is forced to appear through the narrow framework of the "dragon slayer" pattern reinforced by modern technology. To avoid the devastating consequences, the negative pattern needs to be transformed, and the awakening dragon consciousness to be reminded of its angelic nature. The dragons' presence in the manifested world would then reflect the true status of their service to the origins of life (this will be discussed later in this chapter).

The following Gaia Touch exercise was designed to contribute in the process of the freeing dragon powers from the false "dragon slayer" pattern.

GAIA TOUCH EXERCISE TO LEAD
THE DRAGON POWERS TO THEIR ORIGINAL ESSENCE

1. Press the five fingers of your hands into one point to make
   clear that you are dealing with the smallest unit of the
   material world, called by the ancient Greeks "the atom." Your
   hands are positioned in front of your belly. They touch each
   other to form a lemniscate, the symbol of infinity. The archetypal quality of an atom equals infinity. This is why destroy-
   ing one atom represents a threat to the whole universe.

2. Move your hands swiftly apart in a diagonal direction to
   indicate the dangerous process of splitting atoms.

3. At this point the process of transformation starts. Unite your
   hands again, this time in front of your heart.

4. Now open your hands in front of your heart space widely,
   the fingers representing rays of crystal white light. Open and
   close them a few times. The gesture symbolizes the will to
   free the dragon power from the old pattern and to support
   the process of assuming its proper role in the Earthly Cosmos, attuned to the present moment in the Earth's evolution.

5. With a gesture directed to the causal space behind your back,
   the atomic aspect of the dragon powers should be trans-
   ferred from the manifested world to the archetypal world
   where it belongs. Placed there and transformed through the
   power of the heart, the atomic power becomes the base of
   the transformed Earthly Cosmos.

*To visit the dragon house in a systematic way*

If we decide to open the door of human awareness again to the primary powers of Gaia and their dragon consciousness, then we need to create proper images of how their house may be ordered. My geomantic experiences confirm that dragons appear through two different phases—and a third one that will be addressed later.

In the first phase, dragons exist as children of Gaia, representing the first step on the path toward manifesting life in form. In this case dragons represent the primary tool that Gaia has developed to push forward manifestation of her creative ideas. As "children of Gaia," the dragons show in their first phase the seal of the threefold Goddess. One can see the threefold Goddess principle as the source of the three dragon aspects on a painted Viking era rune-stone, dating from 400-600 A.D., from the Baltic island of Gotland.

The image shows the Goddess of Life in the birthing position with two snakes in her hands. They stand for the primeval powers of creation to which she continually gives birth at each successive moment. Above her head are three intertwined dragons representing the consciousness she implements to manifest her creation upon the Earth's surface.

I shall try to translate the three-partite dragon cosmogram from Gotland into logical language. In my attempt I use the usual symbol of the threefold principle of the Goddess expressed through the colors white, red, and black. (This will be explained in detail in the following chapter.)

- *White Dragon* represents Gaia's archetypal ideas, inspiring the initiation of the creative process, leading toward establishing the Earthly Cosmos. The corresponding symbol is the Ouroboros, the White Dragon biting its own tail. It represents the wisdom of Gaia and her creative will to proceed toward creating her own universe.

- *Red Dragon* personifies the primordial powers of Gaia leading all aspects of Earthly creation step by step toward their embodied state of existence. The Red Dragon knows also another face of its existence, appearing as its own tiny fractal, rolled-in within each atom constituting the materialized world.

*The three dragons on a painted stone from Gotland*

- *Black Dragon* is the guardian of Gaia's wisdom and knowledge of how to create the proper mode of existence for worlds and beings that are on their way to manifesting. It knows also the opposite direction, the ways to disintegrate creation and to lead its particles toward the primary state of being. The Black Dragon governs over the beginning and the end of creation.

In the second phase of their approach to the Earth's surface, the structure of the dragon family changes from the triple principle to the one based upon a square, related to the four elements. It becomes more "practical." We can speak of the Fire, Earth, Water and Air dragons. They represent the causal background to the activity of the elemental beings of the four elements:

- *Fire Dragon* is the source of inspiration that moves forward the evolution of nature and the development of cultures.
- *Water Dragon* is a source of life forces and stimulator of their rhythmic flow.
- *Earth Dragon* enables all possible forms of the embodied world to manifest.
- *Air Dragon* enables the flow of the primeval ideas of creation through all the layers of the Earthly Cosmos.

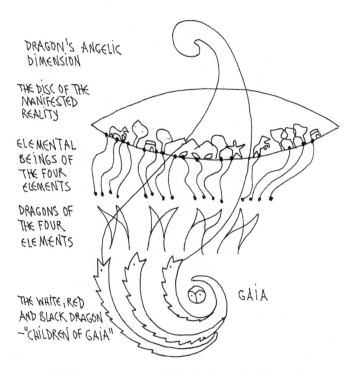

DRAGON'S ANGELIC
DIMENSION

THE DISC OF THE
MANIFESTED
REALITY

ELEMENTAL
BEINGS OF
THE FOUR
ELEMENTS

DRAGONS OF
THE FOUR
ELEMENTS

THE WHITE, RED
AND BLACK DRAGON
—"CHILDREN OF GAIA"

GAIA

*The genealogy of dragons up to the point when the primary forces
of Gaia become embodied in matter*

Supporting the dragons in their service, the elemental beings
of the four elements perform the steps necessary to bring embodiment to landscapes, beings, and phenomena. Each of the dragons
collaborates in different ways with the beings of all four elements.
The input of elemental beings was described briefly during the
first part of our journey. Also, the final incarnation of Gaia's creative hand was mentioned when attention was given to the worlds
of plants, animals, minerals, and human beings.

## Dragons in effect are angelic beings of the Earth

Experiences of my encounters with dragons in different countries
have taught me that dragons, as the embodiment of Gaia's primary powers, know a third phase of their presence in the Earthly
Cosmos. In this case, they appear as a shiny consciousness free
of any specific purpose. As mentioned a few times, the angelic
nature of their consciousness comes forward.

The last chapter of this section of our path will be dedicated to the angelic membranes crisscrossing the universe. There we will get to know the angelic host as the embodiment of the universal consciousness. Yet, relating to the symmetrical governance of the relationship between the holon of the Earth and the holon of the universe, the Earthly Cosmos should know its own angelic sphere. My conviction is that the world of dragons, as presented in the above chapters, *does* represent the angelic dimension of the Earth.

Like angels, dragons traditionally appear as winged beings. Their wings are spiky and solid, mimicking those of reptiles. The wings of the adoring angels belonging to the cosmic networks are of a much softer and lighter nature, like those of birds. The flight of birds through the sky is a relevant symbol to call to memory our consciousness of the vast universe. Ancient pictorial language distinguishes clearly between the angelic conscious-ness of the Earth and the one belonging to the larger holon of the universe.

What does their angelic nature mean in the case of dragons? The angelic phase of dragons reveals them as guardians of the very existence of the Earthly Cosmos. They appear in this role as vast beings of consciousness embracing the Earth, while they are simultaneously present at the core of each atom constituting the manifested body of the Earth and its beings.

## The dragon resonance within the human body

To be true to the concept of integral anatomy, we need also to find the presence of the dragon powers (the primeval powers of creation) and the area of the dragon noosphere working within our human body.

First of all I would like to guide our attention to the belly region, which I perceive as a temple of the primeval (dragon) powers within our body. Their presence can be felt as a large light sphere surrounding and permeating the pelvic cavity. One can imagine it as composed of several layers of golden power streams inlayed with rubies. The presence of the three basic aspects of the dragon—white, red, and black—resonates within

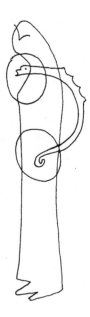

*The creative bridge of the primeval powers*

its layers, together with their angelic quality, primeval power, and archetypal knowledge. I believe that Asian cultures would identify the sphere as "hara."

Following my experience, the sphere permeating the pelvic cavity is not the only place of dragon power within the human body. There exists a second sphere that shows its bluish colors and is positioned in the region of the throat. Both spheres, related to the primeval powers, are interconnected through a resonance bridge positioned in the human back-space.

According to its function, the belly sphere is closely related to the womb and the genitals. The primeval powers of Gaia, contained in the layers of the human dragon sphere, represent the source from which the streams of life are woven permanently.

The upper sphere represents the potentials needed to activate the creative capacities inherent within the human being. Often they are addressed as "the creative powers of the word."

This Gaia Touch exercise related to the primeval powers working within the human body may be of help to you to have your own insights.

GAIA TOUCH EXERCISE TO COME IN TOUCH WITH THE
DRAGON POWERS WITHIN

1. Press palms of your hands firmly upon your ears, the fingers
turned backward and slightly upward, without touching the
skull. If you look at the drawing of Gaia's creative hand on p.
91, then you will understand that by touching the ears with
the palms, the connection to Gaia's matrix is activated.

2. Imagine through this gesture you hold your head firmly in place.

3. With a swift gesture detach your hands from your head, imagining that—not being held any more—your head, in the form
of a light sphere, starts to slowly sink down through the body.

4. Follow the movement of your head's essence downward
with your hands, touching the body, and finally prepare for
it a nice bed in the inner ocean of your belly. Let it rest there
for a while so that concepts and prejudices related to the
dragon powers of Gaia, inherited from your cultural background, can undergo a sorting-out process.

5. After a while, observe your inner world starting from this belly
region. Gather experiences of your belly as a dragon sphere.

6. Imagine bringing the head sphere, tenderly held, up to the level
of your heart. Listen to the quality of the dragon powers here.

7. Finally, bring the sphere of the head to its proper position.
End with your palms upon your ears. This time, all five fingers are touching the skull to make sure that the head is connected again to its functions in the manifested world.

*The role of dragon powers in human creativity*

The temple of the dragon powers pulsating within the pelvic cavity plays a decisive part in the process through which different aspects of human creativity are manifested in daylight reality. Without the support of Gaia's archetypal powers, human creation becomes shallow and of short duration.

The resonance bridge of the dragon power that supports human creativity was mentioned already. As an arched bridge, it ascends from the belly region, through the back space, toward the throat. The dragon powers follow this path when entering the above-mentioned second sphere that pulsates around the throat area. They bring upward the powerful impulses needed to support human creativity. Yet to understand the creative process in all its dimensions, the role of mineral angels needs to be considered too. Their participation in the creative process will be explained in the last chapters of the present part of our journey.

Not long ago I was leading a geomantic workshop in Basel, Switzerland, the city that hides in its name the presence of the bird dragon called "Basilisk." Looking at one of its statues I was inspired to create the following Gaia Touch exercise to stimulate participation of the powers located in the pelvic cavity in the creative process of the throat.

## BASEL EXERCISE FOR TRANSFORMING THE PRIMEVAL POWERS INTO CREATIVE IMPULSES

1. While standing, reach below with your hands into your back space and bring them together behind you; middle fingers are touching. Imagine that from there you establish a contact with the sphere of the primeval forces within your body.

2. Then guide your hands laterally along the body upward, until the middle fingers of your hands touch again, this time in front of your body, more precisely in front of your chest and throat.

3. While moving with your arms upward, bow your head backward so that your throat becomes liberated.

4. Now, when your head is bowed back and the hands are building a circle in front of the throat, you should become aware that the primeval forces of Gaia (so-called "dragon powers") are being transformed into creative powers. Symbolically they are called "the creative powers of the word."

5. After some moments open your hands and stretch them out, thereby the creative powers can flow into your environment to support the creative processes of our home planet.

6. Then, guide the arms laterally down and straighten up your head, in order to repeat the exercise. It should be repeated a few times.

7. Rest for a while after finishing the exercise with closed eyes, to feel what has developed in your body.

# 3

# SOPHIA, THE DIVINE FEMININE

Following the vertical axis of the Earthly Cosmos, we have arrived
to the point of its crossing with the horizontal arm of our guiding archetype, the cosmic cross. At this point our approach to
the world axis turns upside down. Instead of continuing to climb
upward along the vertical axis we will jump to its highest point,
positioned at the center of the universe. From there we will slowly
descend toward the surface of the Earth till our experience of
the world axis is completed. We have been communicating with
Gaia at the bottom end of the world axis, we also need to address
and talk to some being at the upper end. My proposal is to open
our minds and hearts to Sophia, the Universal Wisdom. In Greek
"Sophia" simply means "Wisdom."

## The patriarchal pattern needs to be transmuted first

Considering that it is the most elevated point in the universe, we
should be aware that approaching the upper end of the vertical
world axis can be a dangerous undertaking. Such an image evokes
the illusion that there could be someone sitting upon a throne at
the highest point of the universe who has the mandate to rule over
all and everybody. Such a human projection, in effect, has heavily
distorted the common image of God into the role of a monotheistic
deity to whom the human race should vow absolute obedience.

The time is ripe to detach from the human-created illusion of
a masculine divinity as the supreme ruler over the universe. This
false image has caused much confusion in the patriarchal era of
our history and is continuing to entangle individuals and nations
in neverending conflicts and religiously motivated wars. I think
that it is not possible to approach the upper end of the world axis
in a peaceful way without touching upon this difficult subject.

The exclusive image of the monotheistic God can be transmuted
easily if full attention is given to the feminine face of the divinity.

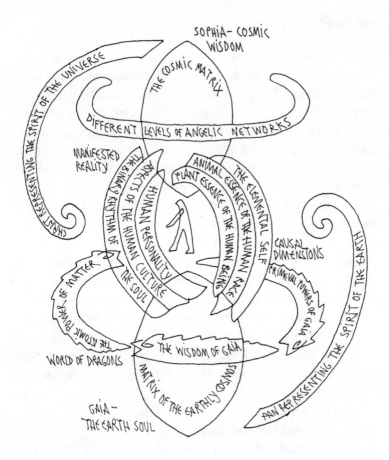

*The human being in relation to the extensions of the Earthly Cosmos*

This does not mean that the masculine God be replaced by a feminine ruler. Such an exchange of roles would make no sense, and the very idea to rule is foreign to the feminine principle. According to its horizontal nature, the feminine principle, if being truly feminine, then is always inclusive, embracing also its opposite pole.

In the previous chapter we got to know Gaia as a creatress of the Earthly Cosmos (Earth Cosmos) and its innumerable beings. At the other end of the World Axis is the home of Sophia, the source of cosmic inspirations and archetypal ideas that seek a way to become living realities. While Sophia descends along the World Axis to become more and more manifest, Gaia is ascending to open its creative potentials to the cosmic inspiration of Sophia.

## The Goddess principle

If God represents the focal point at which all existence and non-existence converge, Goddess stands for the complementary cyclic principle. Unlike the idea of God, Goddess cannot be imagined as a single point but as a permanent cyclic motion. The cyclic movements of the Goddess principle ensure that the idea of divinity cannot be caught in the illusion of a static dominance over the universe, cannot become an agent of separation, and does not support a submissive type of hierarchical order.

The threefold rhythm of the Goddess traditionally is symbolized by three phases of her cycle:

- *The holistic phase of the Goddess*
  The cycle starts as a phase of inspiration with the quality of wholeness and all-connectedness. The holistic phase has diverse symbols such as the figure of the White or Virgin Goddess, the blooming of the spring, the crescent of New Moon.
- *The creative phase of the Goddess*
  During the second phase, the interaction between the feminine and masculine poles comes into focus. Symbolic language refers to the Red Goddess phase, the phase of Full Moon, and the sacred marriage between opposites.
- *The Goddess of transmutation*
  The third phase of the cycle is symbolized by the Black Goddess who represents the dual nature of destruction on one side and regeneration on the other. Individuals and cultures experience the rise of destructive forces that undermine outmoded patterns of social, moral, or political behavior so that proper conditions for the future cycle of growth can appear.

The cyclic principle of the Goddess can be recognized in the background of everyday life as the succession of the mentioned three phases:

- *White Goddess* (virgin) periods are those of inspiration and vision. One feels inspired with new ideas and embedded into the universal whole.
- *Red Goddess* (creative) periods are marked with accentuated creativity. Networks of relationships appear, and with them engagement in social, economic, political, artistic, etc., processes. One

feels useful in the web of life, eager to put one's plans into practice.

- *Black Goddess* (transformative) periods are marked with crisis, with the loss of possibilities to create, often with depressions. The old ways cannot be walked any more. One has to search for new solutions till the next phase of the White Goddess can be felt to appear on the horizon.

The threefold cycle appears at different levels simultaneously, from which two are of decisive importance for our existence here and now. One of them is the level of the Earthly Cosmos where cycles direct the movements of vital processes concerning all of us beings of Gaia, be it in nature or related to cultural developments. The second level is the one of Sophia. With Sophia, we are dealing with cosmic cycles that inspire evolution of the universal space and its civilizations. To get a personal experience of how the two levels are interconnected, the next Gaia Touch exercise (on the following page) can be of help.

## Sophia's mandorla, the seed of creation

There are different venues in which Gaia and Sophia cooperate while representing the two ends of the world's axis. In this interaction, Sophia appears in the role of the Sun Goddess. Through their cooperation, cosmic ideas generated by the wisdom of Sophia can find the proper conditions to germinate on Earth. With the term "cosmic ideas," I think of universal patterns or archetypes within which different potential forms of existence are coded. They can be imagined as seeds of the evolving universal creation.

The earthly and universal poles play different roles in this process. Thanks to the creative capacities of Gaia, the Earth has become one of the precious greenhouses of the cosmic creative process, where the ideas of the future universe, and perhaps of future life systems, are being prepared for their germination.

The seeds of creation are stored below the Earth's surface in the form of specific geomantic phenomena that can be found in different landscapes worldwide. They can be recognized by their characteristic form of a mandorla.

RITUAL TO CONNECT TO GAIA,
THE MOTHER OF LIFE, AND TO SOPHIA,
THE WISDOM OF THE UNIVERSE

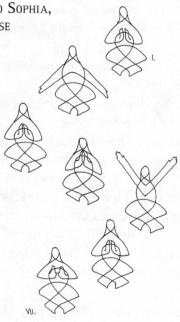

1. This personal ritual can
   be performed sitting or
   standing. Hold your hands
   in a prayer gesture in front
   of the heart center.

2. To begin, start to open
   your hands as you reach
   downward, deep into your
   back space. The palms are
   open and facing forward.

3. By holding your hands
   behind your back at the
   levelof coccyx, you are
   connected to Gaia, the
   Mother of Life.

4. Afterward, your hands
   should return to the prayer
   gesture to invite Gaia's presence
   into the center of your being.

5. Lift the prayer gesture to the level of your throat to connect
   to Gaia's counterpart, the Wisdom of the Universe.

6. Open the prayer gesture with your hands high and wide to
   touch the presence of Sophia—the wisdom of eternity.

7. By bringing your hands together into the prayer gesture in
   front of your chest, her presence will be anchored in your
   heart space.

8. Through the encounter of both aspects of the feminine
   divinity within yourself, you will have touched upon the
   secret of life's origin.

9. Finally, open your hands, holding them close to your body,
   so that reverence for the source of life and awareness of how
   precious it is can shine into the world.

10. The gestures should be repeated a few times before you
    devote yourself to the experience silently.

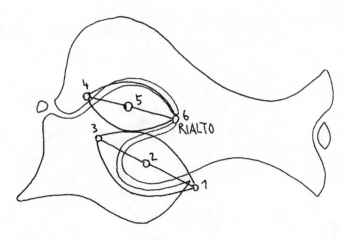

*Two mandorla forms in the urban structure of Venice, with their focal points:*
*San Marco's Water Basin (1), Santo Stefano Church (2), Frari Church (3),*
*Scalzi Church (4), San Giacomo dell'Orio Church (5), Rialto Bridge (6)*

A mandorla is an almond-shaped form that comes into being in the middle of two circles intersecting. It is a spherical form with two pointed ends. As a geomantic phenomenon in a landscape, mandorlas can extend several miles across the landscape. But for Sophia's seeds to manifest in the landscapes of the Earth, the creative potentials of Gaia are needed, including cooperation by human cultures. To create mandorla-form geomantic beads for the cosmic seeds of creation, the collaboration of human intelligence, intuition, and artistic capacity are welcome.

As a consequence, the mandorla-like forms of cosmic seeds can be recognized in the landscape through cultural creations. By positioning historical monuments or places of worship at corresponding places, by specific works of art appearing there, etc., the form of the mandorla in the given landscape or cityscape can be revealed. The above drawing shows two cosmic seeds manifested within the cityscape of Venice. Their presence is marked by the position of important churches along the outline and along the axis of the mandorla.

The following Gaia Touch exercise offers the opportunity to experience oneself within the seed of a mandorla. The double mandorla that comes into being through the exercise is identical

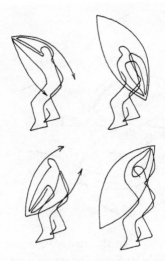

GAIA TOUCH EXERCISE OF PROTECTION WITH A DOUBLE
MANDORLA

1. Squat moderately to be grounded and present.

2. Lift your hands over your head diagonally in front of you
   and put your fingers together to mark the upper corner of
   the mandorla.

3. Draw the arches of the mandorla simultaneously around
   your body, so that at last the fingers come together behind
   your back in a downward movement.

4. Repeat the gesture in the opposite direction without a pause
   in between.

5. Repeat this mandorla-creating movement a few times.

6. At one point, when your hands are positioned behind your
   back close to the ground, lead them around your feet at the
   same level and position the lower front corner of the second
   mandorla.

7. What follows is the drawing of the second mandorla around
   your body in an upward movement till your hands are
   united again behind your head.

8. After you have repeated the second mandorla form a few
   times, stop to enter a period of peace. Be aware that you stand
   within the sphere of your being based upon the four corners
   of the double mandorla. How does it feel to be present within
   the sphere of a seed? You can use the same exercise to create
   a sphere of protection for yourself, your home, etc.

with one's personal holon. This is why the mandorla exercise can be used also to strengthen one's protective membranes.

## The Goddess of Grace

I got to know Sophia as the Goddess of Grace while visiting the pilgrimage chapel of the Black Madonna at Altötting in Bavaria. It is a place of many miraculous healings, as reported by thousands of votive tablets adorning the outer walls of the sanctuary. In the narrow, black-painted inner sanctuary, without any expectation, I knelt down with my hands at my heart in a prayerful gesture to indicate my appreciation of the Goddess's miraculous presence that had been experienced by so many people before me. Yet something happened. I found myself kneeling before the Virgin Goddess as if under an enormous eye that was full of grace. I was urged to bend my hands forward and to open them as one opens a book—without moving them away from my heart.

In the next moment I noticed, in slow motion, that within the universal eye of the Goddess a crystal clear tear was forming. Overwhelmed with the power of the moment I didn't know how to react. Then I realized that in anticipation my hands had already taken the form of a channel. In that same moment the tear dropped into the channel of my hands and began to glide toward my heart. I opened my heart even wider to receive it properly, but to my surprise it did not enter my inner space but instead slid along the surface of my body into the Earth.

Obviously the blessing of the divine grace was not meant for me personally. The message that I felt within the Goddess's tear, as it slid down to the ground, spoke of the divine grace capable of diluting the causes behind the destructive behavior of the human race and its effects. For example, in one of my recent dreams I was shown the gigantic island of rubbish in the middle of the Pacific Ocean. To my surprise, a third of it was eaten away! Whose act could this be?—enabling us to live our lives rather comfortably, even if we have ruined much of the planet's health. There is obviously a flood of divine grace at work—no matter how we would like to call it—that prevents the flow of life from being broken under the weight of human ignorance.

## THE HEALING TEAR OF GRACE

1. Lift your hands in the prayer gesture to the level of your
   heart and let a drop of your compassion (related to the
   person, place, or situation concerned) drop into the space
   between your palms.

2. Bow to the Earth, reaching with your imagination deep
   into the realm of Gaia, the Mother of Life. Create a vessel
   with your hands and ask Gaia for a drop of her forgiveness, related to the distress or insult done to the place or its
   beings.

3. Straighten up and lift the vessel of your hands (containing
   the drop of your compassion and the drop of Gaia's forgiveness) to the heavens and ask for the tear of Sophia's grace.

4. The healing water is now collected. Guide the vessel so that
   in your imagination you direct the healing water toward its
   preconceived goal. Keep a firm heart connection with the
   chosen person or place and its beings to accompany the gift
   of grace on its way there. Continue for a while to be present
   there through the vibration of your open heart.

5. Give thanks. Based on the principles of personal faith and
   telepathy, this ritual works over long distances. It can be
   repeated a few times if needed for different aspects of the
   given situation.

During the years following this experience, I used the Tear of Grace ritual many times while working with groups in places in need of healing. In implementing it, the ritual evolved further. First of all, the circumstances that called for the Tear of Grace required the inclusion of a sign of compassion from the individuals. Secondly, I also included the act of asking Gaia and her beings involved in the given situation for forgiveness. This acknowledged the sorrow felt for forcing them to bear the heavy weight of human stupidity, or even viciousness, upon their backs.

## The Mistress of Dark Powers

Perhaps the most awkward heritage of religions based upon false masculine ideals is the way they deal with the issue of evil. The ancient Persian religion is the most extreme in this sense, presenting the divine universe as a place of constant battle between the God of Light and the God of Darkness. Such a dualistic concept was later adopted by other religions—Christianity unfortunately being one of them. As a result, billions of people are affected by this highly destructive dualistic pattern, which leads inevitably to some kind of confrontation in an intellectual, ideological, or "hardware" war. Striving for what are considered just and good ideals according to the dualistic pattern means at the same time the need to fight against "wrong" ideologies or "evil" people. Our global history of the last few millennia under the predominantly patriarchal rule can be written as a history of permanent wars.

The cyclic principle of the Goddess of Transmutation, based upon the wisdom of Sophia, opens completely different and non-violent possibilities to face the phenomena of the so-called "dark powers":

*Sophia in her aspect as Goddess of Truth:*
Speaking with the vocabulary of the Goddess, "confrontation" should be replaced with the idea of "challenge." Difficult, stressful, or even awkward situations appear in the life of an individual or a nation to introduce some needed changes. If within a creative process, forces appear that obstruct its free flow, then it means something went "wrong" in that process. Perhaps the law of life

was violated in some way and the person concerned was not even aware of it. The resulting aggression of a "counter-force" working against one's intention should not be seen as an act of hate but as a more or less severe reminder to change the proceedings or the actual attitude toward the issue involved. The challenge can come about as a complication in one's personal life or as a large-scale tragedy hitting a whole culture or nation. In such cases Sophia is at work appearing in her Black Virgin phase as the Goddess of Truth. Be attentive to her reminders and the so-called "dark forces" cannot touch you!

### Sophia in her role as Mother Death:

The cyclic principle of the Goddess does not permit that the universe would run upon the track of permanent growth. The idea of ongoing growth is a patriarchal illusion. Phases of growth, in effect, are always followed by phases of decomposition. This process is a venue leading back to the source, and through this in the direction of regeneration. Death does not represent an aggression toward life, rather the opposite. Its role is to lead beings and evolutions over the threshold of death toward their primeval origins. Depriving them of all secondary layers acquired during the phases of embodiment and growth, they are led toward their divine core, so that their essence can be experienced again—also in preparation for the following cycle of resurrection and growth. Have trust in the wisdom of Mother Death!

### Sophia as Seductress opening the path to freedom:

As human beings are beings of free will, nobody in the universe is allowed to push us either collectively or as an individual toward a certain goal, no matter how valuable it is. There are always the best conditions at hand that enable everybody to reach their aspired goal. But human beings are also free to ignore these conditions, and to walk the false ways of illusion and self-deceit. So the Mistress of Dark Powers may direct into life the powers capable of seducing people (or even a whole culture) into entering situations in which their more or less hidden awkward ambitions or diabolical attitudes become magnified, even a thousand times, exposing to everyone their true status. The inevitable following

PEACE MEDITATION WITH THE SWORD OF TRUTH

1. Stretch out your hands to reach deep into the waters of the ocean. Imagine bringing two swords out of the water that represent being at war in their duality.

2. Now fold your hands in a prayer gesture in front of your heart. By this, the sword as a symbol of truth has become whole again.

3. Now integrate the sword into your inner space. Its hilt rests at the point of the perfect presence at the bottom of the belly and its tip touches the root of the nose, where our elemental eye ("fairy's eye") vibrates.

4. Feel the new clarity of the male principle within, whether you are a man or a woman. Take enough time to perceive its beauty. The male principle should return to its true role in life and never again be abused as a warmonger.

5. Confirm your decision by transforming the sword of truth into a sheaf of wheat.

disaster can open eyes and lead toward detaching from illusions. In this way, truth can be taught without taking away the gift of free will from individuals or nations.

### The sword of truth

The above Gaia Touch meditation is designed to transform the dangerous pattern that leads to conflicts and wars. It is a peace meditation inspired by high fairy beings of the island of Mörkö during the International LifeNet gathering in Järna, Sweden, in July 2014. We were shown a possibility of how to transform the matrix of continuous wars into a matrix of peace.

The sword is an ambiguous symbol. Originally the symbol of truth in the hand of the Goddess of Justice, it has been transformed into a tool for killing. When humankind started to make war with one another and to shed blood, the male principle within each man and each woman was defiled.

To end this war fever, it is necessary to convert the sword back into the original symbol of truth and to rediscover the truthfulness of the male principle.

The sword of truth can be understood as an aspect of the scepter of the masculine principle (See pp.111-114).

### The Christ as the masculine face of Sophia

When we asked the question of whether Gaia, as the Soul of the Earth, has a masculine complement, we discovered Pan as her "consort." Representing the Spirit of the Earth, his role is to take care of the well-being of Gaia's creation, spread over the surface of the planet. He is the gardener of Gaia's paradise.

Regarding the Earth's larger holon—the cosmos of the universe—a similar relationship can be intuited between Sophia as the Soul of the Universe and her masculine complement. The problem is to discover his name. Do we know him at all?

The analogy with Pan, in relationship to Gaia, may help us to find out who embodies the Spirit of the Universe. Like Pan performing his role among nature's beings upon the Earth, the masculine aspect of Sophia can be imagined to work with all evolutions and civilizations manifested in all star systems—our solar system and Earth included. There must be some being taking care so that the creative inspirations and will of Sophia are manifested in a way that corresponds to its essence.

It certainly applies to the masculine complement of Sophia, as it does to Sophia herself, that both are understood as forms of cosmic consciousness.

After scanning through historical memory, I came to the conclusion that the presence and activity of Jesus of Nazareth at the beginning of our era in the land of Palestine corresponds to the above criteria. There exist four reasonably authentic reports about his work based upon the memories of his contemporaries, the Gospels.

They claim that the cosmic consciousness we are looking for walked among people for three years, teaching and healing, while embodied in the person of Jesus of Nazareth. Following his inspiration, the human being learned how to reconnect with the matrix of our true self, detaching from false images that the alienated patriarchal ideology projected upon the human race. In regard to his role while embodying that specific cosmic consciousness, the early followers gave Jesus the epithet "the Christ." It comes from Greek "Christos" which means "the anointed one."

Unfortunately, soon afterward a rather stiff religious structure was constructed around Jesus' life and teachings, as well as his mother Mary, that does not realize that Sophia's male aspect does not walk among us to be venerated, but to teach us individually how to reconnect with our true essence. Also, this male aspect is not bound to any person; appearing throughout human history through many individuals before Jesus' times, and later up to the present day interacting with the evolution of human beings and the Earthly Cosmos as the whole. An endless line of saints and teachers of the human race are witnesses—including those in the Eastern world, like Gautama Buddha.

Finally, the presence of the Christ is not a matter of the past at all! At this level, everything is the present. The Christ exists for us today, as much as we are willing to listen to his teaching. For two millennia and more, he has been trying to teach us how to detach from outworn patterns of thinking and finally open ourselves to the inspiration of cosmic Wisdom, to lead us toward dimensions of the renewed Earthly Cosmos.

The relationship between Gaia, Sophia, and Christ is very well presented in a medieval miniature depicting a vision received by the Abbess Hildegard von Bingen (1098-1179). She is one of the most remarkable feminine figures of the Middle Ages: the founder of monasteries, advisor to popes, writer, composer, and herbalist. Her vision shows the dark red figure of Sophia with angelic wings standing on the earth-green body of Gaia, who is enwrapped

*Sophia, Gaia, and Christ in the vision of Hildegard von Bingen*

by one of her dragons, depicted as a snake. As an extension of Sophia's head, the face of the Christ appears, confirming that they represent two faces of one and the same cosmic being. Both heads are depicted as separate, yet at the same time united by a golden ring vibrating between them. The vertical axis of the Earthly Cosmos is presented in Hildegard's vision in a similar way to the last few chapters of this book.

### To experience the Christ as a cosmic presence

If all the phenomena of the Earthly Cosmos are mirrored upon the human body, the same should apply for the presence of the Christ consciousness. Since in this case we are dealing with a presence that is nearly impossible to express in mental concepts, I wish to propose the following Gaia Touch exercise to help achieve personal insights regarding this theme.

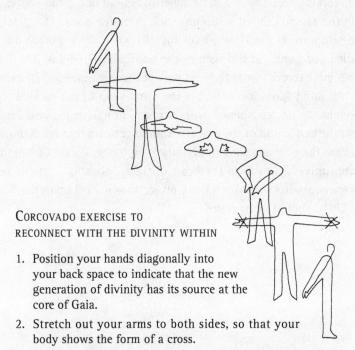

CORCOVADO EXERCISE TO
RECONNECT WITH THE DIVINITY WITHIN

1. Position your hands diagonally into your back space to indicate that the new generation of divinity has its source at the core of Gaia.

2. Stretch out your arms to both sides, so that your body shows the form of a cross.

3. After a while, bend your elbows, so that your palms come to rest on your chest.

4. Become aware that divinity is not only vibrating through the widths of the universe, but also is present at the center of your heart space.

5. Turn your palms around and stretch the fingers outward to indicate that divinity within your heart center is radiating into the world.

6. Move your arms toward the original cross-like position, but this time start the gesture with the back sides of the hands touching each other. This is a gesture of pushing away all the false patterns projected upon the face of divinity.

7. While your hands are now again in the cross-like position, turn the palms toward the world in front of you, and from their centers radiate powers of transmutation to change the false patterns.

8. Then position again your hands into the back space and start the exercise from the beginning. Repeat it a few times and then listen to its echo within yourself.

Working recently in Rio de Janeiro, I could not avoid addressing the famous Christ sculpture with extended arms. The gigantic sculpture is positioned over the city on a steep granite rock called Corcovado. It has become the unofficial symbol of Rio. The Bogomil exercise, from the first part of the book (see p. 72), came to my mind spontaneously. Yet the Corcovado Christ wanted the exercise to be lengthened with two additional sequences. First, that the beginning of the exercise should confirm that the impulse toward the new principle of divinity is no longer coming from the outer universe but from the heart of Gaia. Secondly, that the act of transforming the false human projections loaded upon the face of Christ should be included.

## 4

# ANGELIC MEMBRANES
# — THE COSMIC CONSCIOUSNESS

The present chapters lead us through diverse worlds oscillating along the vertical axis between the two cosmic focuses symbolized by the names of Gaia and Sophia. All those worlds are positioned in symmetrically along the upright axis following the rule "as below, so above." It represents the whole spectrum of forces and beings at different levels of existence engaged in the evolution of the Earthly Cosmos.

May I remind you, dear co-traveler, that we are now on the way to descending the world axis starting at the highest point, the focus of Sophia, and moving toward the manifested world "below." The realm we are entering now is marked by the beings embodying the consciousness of the universe. Tradition calls them by the Greek word *"angeloi,"* meaning "messengers." I wish to lead you through this angelic world. We will examine all the usual preconceptions of angels and visit the meaning of the innumerable membranes of their consciousness throughout the whole universe.

### *Angelic networks are spread throughout the universe*

In the human imagination, angels became winged human-like beings not because their appearance was such, but because of the affinity of human mentality for images. Be aware that the traditional image of the angelic world is contrary to the way I would like to present the angelic sphere. We are not dealing here with lonely birds crisscrossing the universe, but with a multilayered sphere of consciousness permeating the whole universe, its constellations and evolutions settled within planetary systems. If consciousness is involved, then it must be clear that we are dealing with an all-connected network and not with separate units.

Similarly, as dragons hold upright the network of primeval powers upon which the manifested world can be built, the angelic sphere, composed of different consciousness networks, is responsible for the permanent recreating of the causal background of the universe, composed of cosmic ideas, visions, and plans of creation. Each angel is a knot in the weaving of the universal consciousness, representing the precondition that the universe exists as a place of spiritual growth and creative developments, as a place where life can come into existence and evolve at different levels of reality.

Medieval theological tradition knew two different realms of angelic consciousness. The most extended and all-embracing is that aspect of the angelic membranes permeating the universe as a whole, as well as each cell of it separately. The membrane-like networks of Seraphim, Cherubim and Thrones are so delicate that they are capable of permeating all possible phenomena, representing the base of their existence. They hold upright three fundamental qualities as preconditions for the universe to come into being, to exist, and to evolve.

- The carpet of *Seraphim*, spread throughout the universe, holds the pattern of love as the precondition for existence.
- The carpet of *Cherubim*, spread throughout the universe, holds the quality of wisdom as the precondition for development and creativity.
- The carpet of *Thrones*, spread throughout the universe, vibrates with the will to develop the universe in the direction of its manifestation.

At this level the angelic presence can hardly be experienced because it is within each vibration, composing our personal presence and the presence of everything in the universe. Luckily there is a second phase of Seraphim-Cherubim-Thrones presence, which is accessible to human experience. There exist some highly inspired sacred buildings and artistic objects that enable those angelic dimensions to turn inside out and reveal their presence. Examples are the three famous basilicas built by the Renaissance architect Andrea Palladio in Venice: San Giorgio Maggiore, San Pietro di Castello and Il Redentore. (See the following drawing!)

*My vision of the angelic presences in the three basilicas of Andrea Palladio in Venice: Seraphim in the Basilica San Giorgio Maggiore (1), Cherubim in the Basilica San Pietro di Castello (2), Thrones in the Basilica Redentore (3)*

### Angelic hosts are collaborating with the Earth and its evolution

The tradition of the Middle Ages knew also three layers of cosmic consciousness (angelic networks) related specifically to the developments within the Earthly Cosmos:

- *Archai* are focuses of angelic intelligence anchored at specific places on Earth. Each holds certain cosmic qualities that radiate into the environment. These radiated qualities are of importance for the well-being or development of the place or culture evolving there. An example is another place in Venice, where there is the presence of an Archai of Freedom, positioned in the Church San Giovanni Elemosinario near the Rialto. For Venice, as a longstanding republic, the inspiration of freedom was of fundamental importance.

- *Archangels* represent the guiding or inspiring intelligence of a specific epoch, nation, or culture. Their purpose is to permeate the epoch, nation, or culture with the cosmic qualities

GAIA TOUCH EXERCISE TO EXPERIENCE THE ANGELIC
PRESENCE

1. Stand upright. Move your hips in the form of a lemniscate,
   the sign of infinity.
2. After a while, imagine that following the same track of the
   lemniscate is a tiny silvery ball made of liquid mineral, similar to quicksilver.
3. Choose a moment to reach for the ball with your hands and
   lift it to the level of your heart. Perceive. If needed, repeat the
   exercise a few times.

important for its development. As an example, the Archangel Michael should be mentioned. He is considered to be the
inspiring envoy of the present epoch for fundamental planetary change.

• *Angels* are the most known and loved among the three angelic
networks interacting with life on Earth. They are traditionally
known as helpers in all fields of human culture, providing the
qualities of healing, grace, and guidance wherever it is needed.
In the field of geomancy, they are known as landscape angels:
guardians of the original matrix of a given landscape. Their
presence in the landscape is much more subtle than that of
elemental beings. The angelic world and the world of the elemental beings cooperate in the common goal of making life on
Earth a paradise.

*The angelic network within Gaia's lithosphere*

Climbing upward along the world axis we were surprised to discover that the mythical dragons, in effect, represent Gaia's angelic
host.

At this point another surprise is awaiting us. According to my
experience, there also exists a network of angelic beings working within the most solid structures of the Earth's body. We may
speak of these angelic craftsworkers as active within the Earth's
so-called "lithosphere." So besides those networks of the angelic

noosphere collaborating with Gaia, as described above, an angelic host is involved in the evolution of the Earthly Cosmos within the mineral layers of the Earth, the lithosphere.

The lithosphere is a sphere composed of tiny particles of minerals—literally in Greek, "the sphere of stone." The name is normally used for the dense layer of minerals upon which "sits" the manifested body of the Earth's landscapes. Of course it is not as transparent as the atmosphere, yet not so dense that the "lithospheric angels" would not be free to move through it and be creative within its layers. These minerals represent "only" one aspect of Gaia consciousness.

What could be the role of the lithospheric angels within the Earth's crust? My following dream presents an answer:

*I move high through the angelic realms. An inner call directs me to descend and to dig a hole into the ground. The soil is clay, strongly pressed together. At the depth of two feet I find a round white cloth. Looking closely I realize that it is a piece of very fine lace-worked linen, but deteriorating from lying for a long time in the earth.*

Since I received the dream while writing the present chapter on angelic networks, I became instantly alert and began to search for the forgotten angelic community working within Gaia's densest consciousness, called "matter." The fine lacework lost within the dense layers of clay signaled that I was dealing with archetypal powers derived from the universe, yet active within the mineral layers of the Earth.

The deteriorated state of the lace-worked linen tells us that the lithospheric angels were active within the mineral layers of the Earth in a very remote epoch. I believe it was the era of the planet's development, billions of years ago, when its material structures were being prepared for hosting all the different life forms of the present-day biosphere.

In the present epoch of Earth Changes, we are witnessing a similar challenge. Dense matter should be transformed into a sensitive multilayered membrane capable of hosting a pluridimensional space and time structure of manifested reality.

So it makes sense that the lithospheric angels are again called to work.

While leading a workshop in the Italian town of Mantova (south of Verona) in April of 2015, the lithospheric angels presented themselves to me as groups of long golden staffs, approaching the Earth's surface from the widths of the universe to enter the mineral layers of the Earth's body and to perform their task there. Each golden staff had at its spearhead a small perfectly formed dragon's head. This was to make clear that I was being confronted with the elevated angels of the universe, corresponding with Gaia's dragons. Some eastern cultures would call them "cosmic dragons."

The following exercise is an example of how it is possible to cooperate with the lithospheric angels in the present epoch. It is a gift of Mont César, a hillock north of Paris. The sacredness of the site is forgotten, and now being threatened by a vast garbage deposit located at its foot. During a group ritual with the Tear of Mercy, a group of blue angels rose from the Earth's lithosphere offering help. Their transforming power was, in this case, activated for the purpose of landscape healing.

### The role of the lithospheric angels in the human body

To find the resonance of the lithospheric angels within the human body I need to remind you of the light bridge leading across the human back space that connects the workshop of Gaia's archetypal powers in the pelvic cavity with our organ of expression, the throat. The bridge was mentioned at the end of the chapter on dragon consciousness (see p. 124) as supporting the creative powers of the human being to express through the throat.

I was not aware while writing that chapter that the interaction between the primeval powers of the pelvic cavity and the creative capacities of the throat does not come about automatically. Without the cooperation of the cosmic dragon consciousness—as described above in relationship to my Mantova experience—the primeval (atomic) powers of Gaia are not able to support human creativity. They turn round and round in the belly region, unconnected to our mental, spiritual, and emotional activity.

GAIA TOUCH EXERCISE
TO COOPERATE WITH THE
LITHOSPHERIC ANGELS
IN THE TRANSMUTATION
PROCESSES

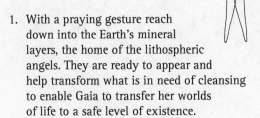

1. With a praying gesture reach down into the Earth's mineral layers, the home of the lithospheric angels. They are ready to appear and help transform what is in need of cleansing to enable Gaia to transfer her worlds of life to a safe level of existence.

2. Lift your body slowly up while you are inviting the Angels of Transmutation to approach the Earth's surface. Express the presence of angels through a gesture imitating the angelic wings (see the drawing).

3. Perform gestures of transformation with your hands in front of your chest, to make clear the purpose for which the angels were called. The gestures resemble the turning of a globe.

4. The turning of the hands finds its peace in a prayer gesture.

5. Then direct angels through the gesture of your hands (still holding the prayer gesture) toward the place where their help is needed. You need to hold the idea, symbol or image of that place in your imagination.

6. Feel free to explore some other possibilities of collaboration with the lithospheric angels—alias the "cosmic dragon powers"—residing within the mineral layers of the Earth.

It is the task of the lithospheric angels within the human body to activate the bridge by which our creativity gets grounded in the immense power of Gaia's dragon consciousness. If that link is missing, then the primeval creative powers stored within the pelvic cavity are imprisoned in their own space and cannot properly support human creativity, symbolized by the power of the creative word. As a consequence, the venue of human creativity becomes so shallow that, with all our activity, we are not capable of co-creating the world at the deeper causal levels. We can introduce changes merely at the surface of the manifested world.

GAIA TOUCH EXERCISE FOR ACTIVATING HUMAN CREATIVE
POTENTIALS

1. Start with the praying gesture positioned in front of your
   throat to indicate your will to work on activating your creative potentials.

2. Move with your arms upward to form a perfect circle in
   front of your throat. While moving with your arms upward,
   bow your head backward so that your throat becomes open.
   (The purpose of this first sequence is to invite the cosmic
   dragon consciousness to enter the process.)

3. Lower the circle created with your arms to position it horizontally in front of the heart, to tune the catalyst power of
   the cosmic dragon (the lithospheric angels) to your body and
   mind system.

4. Next go with your arms even lower around your waist
   (always touching the body) to bring them together behind
   your pelvis, the middle fingers are touching. Through this
   gesture you create resonance with the sphere of Gaia's primeval forces residing in the pelvic cavity. Make a short pause.

5. Guide your hands laterally along the body upward, until the middle fingers of your hands touch again, this time in front of your body, more precisely in front of your chest and throat.

6. While moving your arms upward, bow your head backward so that your throat becomes open.

7. Now, when your head is bowed back and your hands are building a circle in front of the throat, you should become aware that the primeval forces of Gaia (the so-called "dragon powers") are being transformed into creative powers. Symbolically they are called "creative powers of the word."

8. After some moments you should open your hands and stretch them out, thereby the creative powers can flow into your environment to support the creative processes of our home planet.

9. Then guide your arms toward your throat and form again the praying gesture in front of your throat in order to do the exercise again. It should be repeated a few times.

10. Rest after finishing the exercise with closed eyes to feel what has developed in your body.

To work on activating the creative capacities of the throat, I propose this Gaia Touch exercise for transforming the primeval powers into creative impulses as presented at the end of the chapter on dragons.

But in this case, the exercise is expanded to address the bridging power of the lithospheric angels (the cosmic dragon consciousness) to serve as a catalyst between the dragon powers of the pelvic cavity and the creative capacities of the human throat. This is the reason why the movement rising from the pelvic cavity, upward in this new version, are complemented by movement in the opposite direction, inviting the cosmic dragon consciousness to descend in order to then initiate the upward movement.

# INTERMEZZO II

As we make a pause here to look back at the path that we left behind and to ponder over the plans for our future journey, we need to get to know different kinds of keys or codes that will be useful for opening the doors on our path through the coming chapters.

Ahead of us is a most interesting part of our journey, entering the human body and walking among its various extensions and organs.

But first I propose a brief moment to look back at the path we have traveled, using as the key the model of Gaia's creative hand that we got to know in the first part of our journey.

## Gaia's creative hand — the third continuation

I want to now strongly emphasize the fact that I mentioned before that the human hand is a perfect physical manifestation of the principles upon which the Earthly Cosmos is built. It seems as if the Mother of Life attracted the human race into the orbit of her creation so that with the help of our human hands she could embody her creative ideas in the material world. To serve Gaia's purpose, the human hand needed millions of years to develop to the point of perfection that we enjoy today. Do we honor our own hands enough? Do we have the right to use the fractal of Gaia's creative hand to sow death, misfortune, and destruction among our co-human beings and the beings of nature? Is it not so, that the human race is often acting against the essence of our own hands?

In the last two parts of the book we got to know the role of the five fingers that we inherit from Gaia. They stand for the five elements and the consciousness operating in their causal background. Before we continue on our journey we need to become reacquainted with the core of Gaia's hand, its palm.

In the first part of the book we interpreted the palm of Gaia's hand in the form of a triangle encompassing the following faces of Gaia:

- Gaia as the all-connecting soul of the planet
- Gaia representing the divine dimension of the Earth
- Gaia embodying the archetypal matrix of life

Now we need to add to this, another triangle of powers that we got to know along the path in the second part of the book. Without their collaboration there would be no bridge enabling Gaia's ideas of divinity to be translated into the creative processes that make the wonderful garden of the Earth appear in front of our eyes.

The second triangle is a contribution of the vertical world axis:

- Dragons, standing for the primeval powers of the Earth, represent the foundation upon which the building of the manifested world stands
- Mineral angels move processes in the lithosphere that make it possible for embodied life to come into existence from moment to moment
- The elemental civilization of the Earth (in Celtic called "Sidhe") takes care that all beings of Gaia's creation co-exist in peace, mutually supporting each other

I believe that in such a way Gaia's creative hand—manifested in human hands—is presented in all its aspects. But the human being has two hands! Not much can be accomplished with one hand only. Until now, we have only gotten to know the left hand. Where is the partnering right hand?

In effect, climbing along the vertical world axis we ascended from the left hand, Gaia's hand, to the creative right hand, the hand of Sophia. If the four fingers of Gaia's hand symbolize the four Elements, then their counterparts upon Sophia's hand would be the four angelic networks presented in the last chapter of part two. The three knuckles of Sophia's thumb can be identified with the angelic consciousness that permeates the whole universe, into the last atom. Tradition calls the three knuckles: Seraphim, Cherubim and Thrones. Without their participation in the cosmic creative process, the right hand would be useless.

The image of the complementing hands of Gaia and Sophia embodied in human hands is the ultimate call to change radically our relationship toward our own hands. In the modern world of digitalization, our hands, which should be creative hands, tend to become redundant. A multitude of unemployed or wrongly employed human hands are longing to be implemented as creative tools. We should not allow the creative potential of the human hands to dissipate.

### The passage through an interdimensional portal

Walking the horizontal and then the vertical path of the cosmic cross, we got to know different dimensions of the human being, seen in the context of the Earthly Cosmos. We arrived at the point where the two arms of the cross intersect, where it seemed that our journey was finished. The "dry" point of the intersection does not promise any further steps to be taken. For the rational mind, it is equal to the sign "No Way."

Geomantic knowledge understands the point of such a crossing in a different way. Like an hourglass, it can be imagined as a doorway to other dimensions, a so-called "interdimensional portal." An interdimensional portal is a zero point through which it is possible to glide into dimensions of existence that vibrate beyond the scope of the rationally structured world.

How does one get through the zero point?

Luckily, during the aforementioned workshop that took place in Brazil, one of the gigantic megaliths of Rio de Janeiro, the most famous of them, the so-called "Sugar Loaf," taught me an exercise that can be used as a key to pass through the zero point of an interdimensional portal. My hands were lifted and positioned at each side of my body. They were then lead forward in an arched form till the palms bumped into one another. I had arrived at the zero point. There I had to perform an unlocking gesture, continuing the arched path with both hands, this time in the form of a widely opening gesture.

Before starting the movement, I was present in the fixed reality of the mentally organized world. On the opposite side of the portal a surprise waited for me. It was a colorful butterfly floating in the

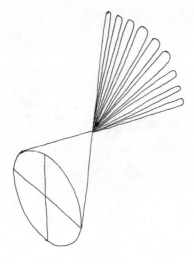

*The sand clock form and zero point of an interdimensional portal*

air in front of my nose. My intuition heard the invitation "follow me." Without hesitating I started to run after it. It turned out to be an unexpectedly long journey. We climbed over eight mountain ranges and crossed the nine valleys extending between them. The butterfly was fluttering the entire journey, not far from my nose, enticing me to continue.

Unfortunately I had little time to look around. To not lose my guide, I had to hurry. Yet I realized that each valley presents another extension of the multidimensional Earth. My mind was not yet capable of providing the images needed to recognize the separate worlds that I passed through during the different phases of the journey.

What was clear to me is that I was led through the nine-dimensional Earthly Cosmos, existing beyond the rational framework of our daylight reality, and beyond the materialized world map.

Before proceeding with the story, I wish to present here the Gaia Touch the exercise inspired by the Sugar Loaf:

### The twelve-dimensional blueprint of the Earthly Cosmos

Arriving safely home in Slovenia, I was eager to repeat the journey through the world dimensions in a meditative way. I wanted

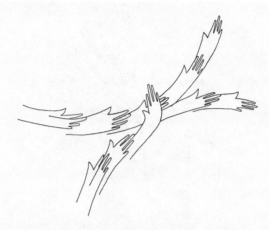

GAIA TOUCH KEY TO GLIDE THROUGH AN INTERDIMENSIONAL
PORTAL

1. Lift your hands, positioned at both sides of your body, as far
   from the body as possible. Palms are in a vertical position.

2. When your intention is clear within yourself, lead your
   hands forward, horizontally, in an arching form till they
   bump into one another. You arrived at the zero point.

3. Without hesitating, you need now to perform the gesture of
   unlocking a door. While one hand moves into the vertical
   position, the other one stays in the horizontal. (Both palms
   touch each other during the unlocking gesture!)

4. In the next instant, the hand that moved vertically returns to
   its horizontal position and both hands continue their arched
   path forward in an opening gesture.

5. After the brief pause, follow the same path backward toward
   your body. This time using both hands in an unlocking gesture.

6. With your hands finishing back to the starting position, go
   on repeating the exercise. One needs to repeat this a few
   times so that the guardian of the portal can recognize it
   and react properly. (The gate may not open if the guardian
   realizes that you are not ready to confront the challenges
   perhaps waiting at the other side of the portal.)

enough time to examine the lands of which I had initially only
caught a glimpse. A bitter disappointment followed. Arriving at the
other side of the portal, I met a mourning woman clothed in grey

robes in the midst of a graveyard. What did this mean? Looking around, I realized that I found myself in the middle of a wasteland. In despair I turned inwardly to my guide from the fairy worlds, who had initially appeared in front of my nose as a butterfly.

Fluttering in front of me, the butterfly again led me through the interdimensional portal. Instead of "outward" toward the unknown spaces, I was led through the inner dimensions of my own human being. This time a bluish colored space, structured like a crystal, opened graciously in front of me. I knew that if I continued walking in this direction, then my wish to discover different dimensions of my human essence would be fulfilled.

The two contradictory experiences made me understand the bitter truth. The path toward the multidimensional reality, for millennia used by shamans and esoteric teachers, has lost its credibility. It was misused too often by religious fanatics and political elites secretly craving power. Its spiritual treasures were stolen, and perhaps substituted with illusionary images that can mislead seekers of truth.

Meanwhile Gaia/Sophia wisdom has opened another path to approach the various dimensions of the universe. This path is attuned with the new constitution of the Earthly Cosmos. It leads through the halls of one's own multidimensional body, which represents a holographic unit of the Earthly Cosmos (its smallest holon), no less complete or wonderful than Gaia/Sophia's universal creation.

## A spherical model of the human being

Traveling first through the horizontal and then through the vertical arm of the cross archetype, we arrive at a point where we have to pass through an interdimensional portal to be able to continue our journey. As reported before, I bravely glided through the portal, arriving at a differently organized reality. This reality is based upon a new blueprint of the Earthly Cosmos, and consequently upon a new spherical matrix of the human being.

To translate this new blueprint into a logical language, I use the system of a 12-dimensional space structure. I decided to work with this system after I heard a lecture by the late German physicist and mathematician Burkhard Heim in Cologne in 1989. His 12-dimensional space model, proved through mathematical calculations, corresponds perfectly to my experiences of working in the subtle dimensions of the landscape. I do not implement it in its mathematical version, but translated into my practical experiences. I wish to briefly present the 12-dimensional model to serve as another key to understanding the multidimensional body of the Earth, of the human being, and other beings as well.

The model is composed of three main sections:

*Dimensions relating to manifested space and time realms:*
- Dimensions 1-4 relate to the human being and other beings or phenomena manifested in matter (width, length, height, and time).
- The 5th dimension encompasses the realm of the vital powers (bio-energy) and their networks. It is the level that makes the human and other manifested beings appear as living beings of the Earth.
- The 6th dimension corresponds to the consciousness sphere. At this level beings are participating in the planetary noosphere.

*Dimensions relating to the causal background of manifested phenomena:*
- The 7th dimension is the first one belonging to the causal world. It is the home of the parallel worlds of Gaia: the ones of plants, animals, minerals, and human beings, together with the world of ancestors and descendents, in one sphere.
- The 8th dimension is the realm of the archetypes and of the general matrix related to all aspects of the Earthly Cosmos. The rosette of the human individuality is also located here.
- The 9th dimension reaches beyond the holon of the Earthly Cosmos, touching the universe as a whole. The human being takes part as a subject of the universal evolution.

*Dimensions touching on the divine nature of the Earth and the universe:*
- The 10th dimension is the first one to relate to the divine realms. An example would be the divine decision to choose a path toward a universe embodied in different galaxies, star systems, causal and manifested worlds.

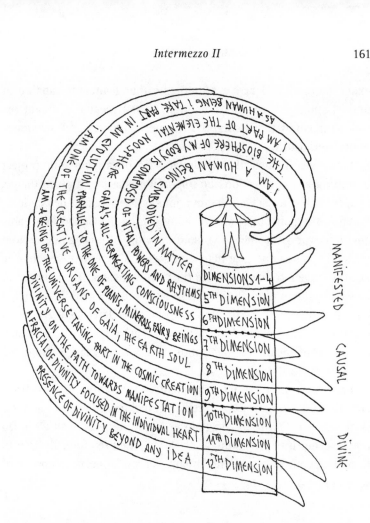

Dimensions labeled within the figure: DIMENSIONS 1–4, 5TH DIMENSION, 6TH DIMENSION, 7TH DIMENSION, 8TH DIMENSION, 9TH DIMENSION, 10TH DIMENSION, 11TH DIMENSION, 12TH DIMENSION. Right-side labels: MANIFESTED, CAUSAL, DIVINE.

Spiral text: AS A HUMAN BEING I TAKE PART / I AM PART OF THE ELEMENTAL NOOSPHERE – GAIA'S ALL-PERMEATING CONSCIOUSNESS / I AM A HUMAN BEING EMBODIED IN MATTER / THE BIOSPHERE OF MY BODY IS COMPOSED OF VITAL POWERS AND RHYTHMS / I AM ONE OF THE CREATIVE ORGANS OF GAIA, THE EARTH SOUL / IN AN EVOLUTION PARALLEL TO THE ONE OF PLANTS, MINERALS, FAIRY BEINGS / I AM A BEING OF THE UNIVERSE TAKING PART IN THE COSMIC CREATION / DIVINITY ON THE PATH TOWARDS MANIFESTATION / A FRACTAL OF DIVINITY FOCUSED IN THE INDIVIDUAL HEART / PRESENCE OF DIVINITY BEYOND ANY IDEA

*A spherical model of the 12- dimensional blueprint*

- The 11th dimension brings a surprise. Instead of reaching toward greater distant regions, the opposite is true. As a representative of the human race, I recognize divinity abiding within my heart system.
- The 12th dimension relates to divinity beyond any idea that could be expressed in words.

## The language of dreams

In my work I often get help through my dreams. Dreams are a form of storytelling. When the rational mind does not understand a complex issue, the explanation might be narrated to the ego in the form of a dream story. This happens to me often in exact succession. I arrive at a theme that I am not capable of understanding. If fortunate enough, then I receive a dream the following night that explains it to me in images and accompanying sensations.

It can also happen that while working on a geomantic project or writing a text I overlook an important aspect of a given theme. In such a case, a relevant dream points out my limited perception.

From my point of view, dreaming can be developed in a valuable dialogue with one's own soul or with spiritual guides whom the soul can call upon for help. To develop it as a creative tool one needs to take into consideration the whole process. Dreams need to be written down after awakening so as not to lose details. Also, the logical structure of the dream has to be considered as it relates to processes in the dreamer's daily life or creative work. The next step is the use of meditative perception to get more clarity about the message of the dream.

From now on, I will more frequently inform you, dear co-traveler, about the dreams that I receive parallel to writing, so that their stories may help you to come closer to the subjects dealt with. Do not take my interpretations as the only interpretation. Be free to formulate your own versions. Dreams represent a text composed of several layers.

# PART III

# WALKING THROUGH
# THE HUMAN BODY

# 1

# VISITING THE HOME OF THE PERSONAL ELEMENTAL BEING

I welcome you to the beginning of the third part of our journey. I would like to remind you, dear fellow traveler, where we actually are. Imagine us standing in front of the portal leading to the inner spaces of the human body, in front of the door leading to the body's "underground."

From the logical point of view, our intention to enter is senseless. The body's tissue is too dense to allow us to walk through to discover its inner constitution. Luckily there are keys—some of them presented in the Intermezzo II—that make such kind of travel possible. They are able to grant to us the freedom to move through the body's underground levels. Obstacles encountered that the rational mind fears, cease to exist.

*Where is the door to enter the body's underground?*

In the Intermezzo II we learned how interdimensional portals work. They represent doorways to pass from the fixed reality of the space and time dimension in which we presently abide to the open spaces of the multidimensional world.

This raised the question of where the proper portal that leads us into our body's inner spaces is located. My intuition pointed, without hesitation, toward the lower end on my breastbone.

One can see the breastbone as complementary to the backbone. Together with the clever architecture of the ribs, the breastbone holds the space needed for the complex human heart system to manifest—we will visit this fascinating space a bit later. Similar to the backbone, the breastbone has its "coccyx," in the form of its arrowhead-like lowest segment.

The entrance to the inner worlds of the body can be found a few inches behind the pointed lower end of the breastbone. Here exists the interdimensional portal leading from the 6th to the 7th dimension—according to the model of the 12-dimensional space presented in Intermezzo II. If dimensions 1-6 represent the manifested world of the physical body with all its organs and functions, then the 7th dimension represents their causal background. In the realm of the 7th dimension the subtle forms and rhythms are coded, according to which the living and breathing human body organism manifests in each successive moment. From here it draws its vitality, health, and beauty.

The point of entrance into the inside world of the body cannot be missed if one starts with one's attention far behind the back and proceeds from there in the direction of the pointed end of the breastbone. Departing from that pointed end, waves expand in a rhythmical way through the body. What is the meaning of this pulsation?

### The personal elemental being is identical to "the body intelligence"

Entering the body through the door behind the lower end of the breastbone means that first we will meet its "doorkeeper," sometimes called "the body intelligence." We met this in a previous chapter as the personal elemental being. The waves departing from the point of his focus behind the breastbone are the expression of his attention, given to all the many extensions of the human body.

During our first visit to the world of the elemental beings we got to know that all the beings manifested upon the Earth cooperate with their elemental helpers. Elemental beings can be understood as an offshoot of Gaia consciousness, working with the vital phenomena upon Earth's surface. Gaia needs such an intelligent and relatively embodied community of helpers to be able to take care of her creation, manifested at different levels of the Earth's vital organism.

The personal elemental being helps its human companion to move through a life-span, starting from a certain point before conception (we touched upon the subject in the first part of the journey) all the way to our departure back to the worlds of the soul. During this entire time span, the personal elemental being abides within our water body, moving freely through the waters of our personal ocean.

The work done by the personal elemental being can be imagined as a tiny drop of silvery substance that at each successive moment falls into the pool of our water body. The particle then passes through our body in the form of a particular vibrational wave. It is this wave that touches all the organs of our body at the different levels of existence, checking that they are in tune with their matrix and adjusting as needed. There is not a single moment that the personal elemental being's wave of attention is not focused on the layers of our organism, performing the services needed. Like a constantly beating heart, it would be a disaster if the personal elemental being abandoned his duties for one single instant.

In order to emphasize the importance of the personal elemental being—our body intelligence—I wish to add a few further points:

- Connected to the matrix of the Earthly Cosmos on one side, the personal elemental being cooperates on the other side with the individual archetype of the given person. As such, it represents a bridge between the two sources of our identity. We are beings of the Earthly Cosmos and at the same time a soul with an individual destiny and purpose in the evolution of the universe.

- The personal elemental being is responsible for the proper energy tension of our body. If the tension were to drop under a certain limit, then the life of a person would be endangered. The same is true in the opposite direction. A person would get burned in an instant if the energy tension gets too high— such cases are documented.

- The personal elemental being protects the greatest treasure stored in the human body, our complex heart system.

The personal elemental being protects the greatest treasure stored in the human body, our complex heart system.

The expression "personal elemental being" can be misleading if thought of as our personal servant. Not at all! It is also not true that the personal elemental beings see humans as possessions in any way. Rather they see us as an expression of Gaia consciousness

*The personal elemental being interacting with the human individuality*

that needs to be cared for like a butterfly, a flower, or the health of a landscape.

## A general blockade of the personal elemental being

In the previous chapter on elemental beings, it was stated how difficult it is for the personal elemental being if people are not working on dissolving old traumas and blockages deposited in their bodies. The frozen energy kept there does not allow the elemental being to move freely through those places in our organism. It is forced to avoid those spots in tuning the body's organs to the matrix of their perfect state of being. As a result, organs located in blocked places may get out of tune and become seriously ill. To avoid this danger, one is encouraged to persistently work to transform one's "old stuff."

Besides our personal obstacles hindering the work of the personal elemental being, there exist blockades that concern the human race as the whole. They were inflicted upon the human race by manipulating the blueprint of the human being that is stored in the memory of the Earth and within each human being. The manipulation was possible because the human race has forgotten its role in Gaia's plan: to transform our home planet into a house of truth and a loving community of its inhabitants.

The general blockade, not allowing the elemental being to touch fully upon the human head, is particularly troublesome to me. It seems that through this manipulation, a specific part of the human brain has been hidden from the supervising eye of the personal elemental being. Instead of becoming beings of wholeness, humans could be pushed into the position of become beings with a "dry" (rationally limited) head.

The sneaky source and the dangerous consequences of the blockade were explained to me through the following dream:

*I see a large group of men with funny hats on their heads, training horses to move in a certain way. My interest is drawn to one of them. With one hand, he holds his horse by the rein. In the other hand—also at the level of the horse's head—he holds a plastic bottle two thirds full with a red liquid. I notice that the bottle is wrapped in transparent cellophane. My guess is that it might contain wine. I realize how difficult it is for him to train the horse and at the same time to hold the bottle in one hand. Why doesn't he leave the bottle at the side of the training arena and go there when he is thirsty?*

*As if answering my question he lifts the bottle to the level of his mouth. But instead of drinking from it, the opposite happens. I see a jet of red liquid emanating from his mouth directed into the strange bottle!*

The horse trainers represent modern human beings working on training their intellect. This could be normal for conscious beings, except the mysterious bottle hints that something is wrong. The fact that the bottle is wrapped in almost invisible cellophane indicates something being hidden from human awareness. What is it?

The awkward "spurting" of the red liquid into the bottle lays the mystery bare. My interpretation is that the flow of liquids, carrying the awareness of the personal elemental being upward through the body, is not free to pass the portal of the throat and to circle through the head area. An arm of the flow is diverted at the peak of the throat, trapping it "in the plastic bottle." Remember that the personal elemental, to perform his job, must follow the natural flow of our water body.

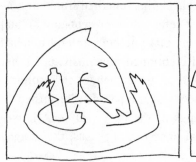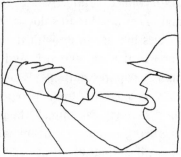

*The dream with the horse trainers*

The fact that the bottle was held as close to the horse's head as possible hints at which aspect of human intelligence is blocked: that aspect of our mental capacities inherited from our animal ancestors.

Which intelligence, inherited from our animal ancestors, could be blocked at the level of the throat? Do you remember our discussion of gifts that we received from the animal kingdom? Among them, the quality of the instinctive consciousness was mentioned. Thinking instinctively enables us as humans to connect with the flow of life and its possible turns within ourselves and in our environment. The capacity to think in the instinctive way represents the proper antidote to rational logic. It is needed to prevent the human mind from becoming frozen into rational one-sidedness.

Rational one-sidedness ignores the causal levels of existence. Its logic is trapped upon the surface of the manifested world like a fish on dry ground.

### The elemental being and the integral path of thinking

The dream of the horse trainers hints that the personal elemental being is the key enabling humans the capacity to think in an integral way. Further, that the capacity is connected to the knowledge that the human race received from the animals. From scientific sources we know that there exists a part of the human brain connected directly to the backbone, inherited from our animal ancestors. Yet this does not refer to the present-day animal species but has to do with the animal ancestors briefly touched upon in the Intermezzo I. As I mentioned previously, our inner animal requires during this time of great changes to reconnect with its ancestors from the epoch "of the paradise." I presented them as mythical animals, beings of the fairy realms. A horse-like being is among our animal ancestors: Pegasus, the winged horse, inspiring the art of poetry.

Returning to the above dream and trying to translate its negative connotation into a positive message, I propose following conclusions:

- The personal elemental being has the key to the so-called "reptilian brain," the seat of the integral principle of thinking developed by Gaia and shared among all beings of the planet, invisible and visible.
- The elemental being uses, in this case, the interdimensional portal located between the top of the backbone and the skull. The door located there leads from the body's 7th to the 8th dimension. The 8th dimension represents the realm where the archetypes of the integral mentality are stored, at the same time representing the matrix of the holistic existence.
- The integral mentality is something different from the synergy that comes into being when both brain hemispheres cooperate. The integral way of thinking functions without the need to think, so to say. Thinking, in this case, is identical with existing. "Thinking by being" is the phrase.

It is obvious that the blockade of the human capacity to think in an integral way is not a random matter. One feels eager to work on dissolving this dangerous obstacle. How to do the healing work? There are obviously two steps that need to be done. First, we must assure that the streams of our water body are free to make the whole body moist. Second, the link connecting us to the archetypes, guarded by our animal ancestors, needs to be renewed.

The following corresponding exercise is a combination of two Gaia Touch exercises from the second part of the book:

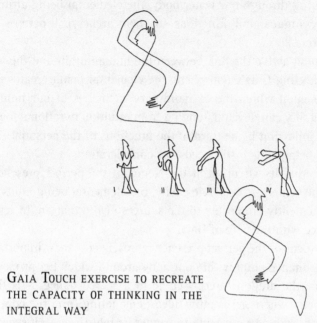

GAIA TOUCH EXERCISE TO RECREATE
THE CAPACITY OF THINKING IN THE
INTEGRAL WAY

1. Perform for a while the exercise for activating the streams of your water body, presented in the chapter on Gaia and the resonances of oceans upon our body (p. 109).

2. Then use the first sequence from the "Gaia Touch exercise to embody new proportions between different aspects of the human being." (p. 88) Use points 1 and 2, featuring the inner animal doing three steps backward to reconnect with the animal archetypes.

3. Work for a while on both of these aspects by exchanging the two sequences. Then calm down and concentrate at the place where your backbone touches the skull. How does it feel?

## *The elemental being holds a permanent link to the sources of life*

It is not by chance that on entering the body's inner worlds, we first met its elemental being. Standing for the body's consciousness, the personal elemental being holds the three basic conditions for a human being's ability to appear in manifested form and lead an incarnated life on Earth. We covered two of these already:

- Flowing through our water body, the elemental being attunes body organs and functions to their archetypal pattern or matrix.

- Holding active the link between the human brain and the all-connecting Gaia's noosphere, the elemental being creates the base upon which the extraordinary capacities of our human mentality can develop, ranging from intuition to rational logic.

The following is the third of the functions of the personal elemental being, which still needs our consideration.

- Centering its attention at the "focus of the perfect presence" at the center of the pelvic cavity, the elemental being holds us permanently connected to the sources of life that are in resonance with the core of Gaia.

The focus of the perfect presence represents the most important Gaia resonance point within our body around which her primeval powers—the dragon forces—circle in a sacred dance. It is this Gaia focus, where her creative ideas, emanating from the core of the Earth, arrive in our body to trigger its rebirth in each successive moment. Even more, the focus of the perfect presence represents the point of connection to Gaia's creative hand. Being led through the Earthly Cosmos by Gaia's hand allows us to act and create within the Earthly Cosmos, while avoiding causing pain or limiting the freedom of other beings that are a part of the same web of life.

In the case of the focus of the perfect presence, the elemental being has the task of holding open the interdimensional portal leading from the manifested realms of the Earthly Cosmos (dimensions 1-6) to its causal realms, including the world of the ancestors and descendents (dimensions 7-9). After he has opened that door we can start our more or less happy journey through the halls of the manifested world—till the door is closed in the moment of death. After death, the human being has to retreat to the sphere of ancestors and descendents. I mention this to underline how important the portal of the perfect presence is.

This focus of the perfect presence is also of decisive importance for the quality of human life. How much we are present decides how fulfilled (or lost) our life is. Remember the conversation on animals and their capacity to be present at each moment? This

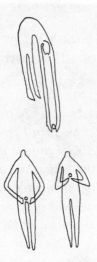

GAIA TOUCH EXERCISE TO STRENGTHEN THE LINK WITH
THE FOCUS OF THE PERFECT PRESENCE

1. Bow down deeply. Imagine reaching with your hands deep down until you touch the core of the Earth.

2. Take a holographic piece of the essence of the Earth in your hand and knead it into a little ball. Imagine it as a seed within which the life-giving powers of Gaia are imprinted.

3. Raise yourself up while imaging that you carry the seed upward.

4. Hold it silently at the center of your pelvic cavity to strengthen the focus of your perfect presence.

5. Lift the little ball even further up to the level of your heart. Open it there with the gesture of an opening a seed to feel what the presence of Gaia tells you in the that moment.

6. Now you can distribute its qualities throughout your auric field, and into the environment and the world.

7. Repeat the exercise a few times consecutively.

allows that they can open the treasury hidden within each moment of the universal life and enjoy its gifts. Human beings succeed only in rare moments to be fully present. Most of the time we roam with our thoughts through the past and future of our abstract mind. Instead we should re-learn to be anchored consciously at the focus of perfect presence at the center of our pelvic cavity.

### The personal elemental master

A short impressive dream made me aware that there must be a further aspect of the personal elemental being that is foreign to my consciousness:

*I find myself standing inside a cave in front of a heavy door made of stone—a two-winged door. Then I realize that behind the door bright golden light is shining. I can see it penetrating through the narrow fissure between the heavy door and the wall of the cave. Asking what the source of this mysterious light could be, I get an instant answer. An elemental being pushes his prolonged nose through the fissure at the bottom of the door. How astonished I am!*

The dream tells me that there exists another quality of the personal elemental being, one that is foreign to my mind. The golden light behind the heavy door can be seen as a hint that the being pushing its nose through the fissure knows dimensions that are beyond my imagination.

I think of the role of the personal elemental being as a master that knows all the secrets, advantages, and dangers of existence within the Earthly Cosmos. The personal elemental being could be labeled in that role as our "fairy master." He accompanies the human being in the back space of our causal world as a lifelong equal partner. He helps the human being to orientate among all the numerous levels and dimensions of the Earthly Cosmos that I have tried to describe along our path through the integral human body.

Our path through a given lifetime would be much easier if we were to re-learn conversing with our good partner, our personal elemental master, from the fairy world.

Luckily the elemental master—at least in my experiences—is a being of humor. This was also obvious in the way he showed himself in the dream, pushing his large nose through the fissure at the bottom of the door. I believe that as a tolerant teacher he does not take offense at the stupidity of human beings related to the marvelous extensions of life.

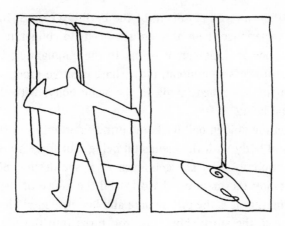

*The image from the dream of the personal elemental master*

## Reconnecting with the personal elemental master

What follows is a body cosmogram to help reconnect with the personal elemental being. This Gaia Touch exercise is a gift of the mighty fairy beings from the island of Mörkö in the Baltic Sea.

The body cosmogram reflects the story of the three iron rings that are said to oppress the human chest, not allowing our heart to beat with its full potential. The brothers Grimm recorded the story in the 18th century in the Frog King fairy tale.

The Frog King story brings to attention the awful and unjust relationship of human beings to the elemental kingdom, specifically to their personal elemental being, who is presented in the story as a frog.

The story begins with the princess whose golden ball falls into a deep and muddy well. It is an image of how the human soul feels when incarnated into the conditions of matter. It seems to the soul that the wholeness that it knows from the worlds of its origin is lost forever like the golden ball being buried in the mud of the well.

The Frog King appears as the representative of the elemental world, assuring the princess that with his help she can find within the incarnated world the same beauty and perfection she is longing for. Indeed, the manifested earthly realms are not less perfect than any other sphere of the Earthly Cosmos. But to be able to experience them as such, she needs to cooperate lifelong with the personal elemental being. In the language of the fairy tale, the princess should eat, play (share creative processes), and sleep in the same bed (abide in the same body) with the frog/ elemental being.

To get the golden ball back, the princess promises to share her world and body with the elemental being, but forgets her promise intentionally after she gets back what she desires. Similarly, people enjoy the manifested world and the house of their body, forgetting that it is the gift of Gaia and her elemental kingdom.

To make the story short, the frog turns into the figure of a prince so that the princess can realize that the ugly frog is equal to her majesty in his status. On the way to their marriage, three iron rings break one after another upon the chest of their coachman, called Iron Henry—a representative of the modern human being. The three iron rings, which prevent the qualities of the human heart from expressing fully, symbolize three blockades that do not allow us to connect heart to heart with our elemental partner:

- First iron ring—denying ourselves as beings of the Earthly Cosmos.
- Second iron ring—humiliating other beings of the Earth to the point of using them as slaves or even declaring them as non-existent.
- Third iron ring—chaining all beings and aspects of the manifested world to the narrowness of our mental projections, preventing them from expressing their wholeness in the framework of the world dimension controlled by human culture.

The following Gaia Touch exercise relates, on one side, to the three focuses of the personal elemental being mentioned above. On the other side, it uses the three finger knuckles of the human hand to break the three iron rings one after another.

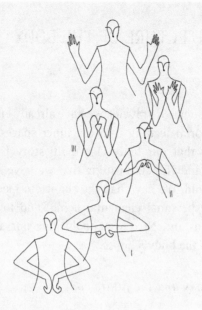

GAIA TOUCH EXERCISE TO RECONNECT WITH THE PERSONAL
ELEMENTAL MASTER

1. Go with your hands deep down to the bottom of the belly to
   connect with the focus of the perfect presence. Fingers are
   clenched, hands turned back to back.

2. Then move higher to the level of your plexus to break the
   first iron ring (I). It is symbolized by the first knuckle of your
   fingers. The fists touch at the first row of knuckles.

3. Move a bit higher to the level of the pointed lower end of the
   breastbone to break the second iron ring (II). The fists touch
   at the second row of knuckles.

4. Move your hands to the level of your heart, to break the third
   iron ring (III). The fists touch at the third row of knuckles.

5. Now the iron rings are all cracked. Without moving the
   arms, open the fists as a flower opens.

6. Then open the arms to announce to the world that the heart
   of the human being is again open for the beauty of the
   Earthly Cosmos and all its beings.

7. Repeat the exercise a few times so that its message can settle
   into the body and the surrounding landscape.

8. It is possible also to go in the opposite direction, breaking the
   iron rings from above downward.

# 2

# THE ARCHITECTURE OF THE BODY

To remind you, dear co-traveler, we have already entered the inter-dimensional portal leading into the inner spaces of the human body. Imagine that our body is a multi-story house, inhabited by the human individual, meaning that we have already stepped over its threshold. We have had the chance to meet the keeper of the house, the personal elemental being, and to experience his different dimensions. Next we should give our attention to the architecture of the body's house.

*The present body and the future body*

Before we start to explore the materials composing the house of the human body and to observe the principles of its construction, we should clarify our point of interest. On our journey we are not interested in getting to know all that is known of the human race, to the last detail. We are not interested in the body's skeleton, the logistic of the muscles, or the function of the skin. We even do not intend to deal with the esoteric insights complementing the rational knowledge, i.e., the etheric layers of the body, the chakras, its bio-energetic organism, etc. All this is important of course, yet it is already known; and such information can be easily located in a library or on the Internet.

What interests us on our journey is the human body beyond the limitations inflicted upon it by the rationally organized way of thinking and formulating reality. Our matter of interest is in the "future body." I speak of the bodily constitution that is mainly hidden from our awareness, yet becomes revealed step by step through the transforming process triggered by the present-day Earth Changes.

The following dream can help us understand why the transmutation process does not demand changes in consciousness only, but works in a transformative way upon the body:

*The dream of the alienated city*

*I roam through Venice, unable to find the church San Francesco della Vigna. I can not understand why it eludes me, since I have visited it alone and with groups many times. Also I realize that Venice is different this time, looking like a neglected suburb. Noticing two young men in a courtyard I ask them where San Francesco is. They answer in an unknown language that is far from Italian. Obviously they do not know where San Francesco della Vigna is, even though it is one of the most known churches in Venice.*

*Searching, I arrive at the shore of the lagoon that surrounds Venice. There a surprise waits for me.*

*The water of the lagoon, always a bit dirty, this time looks absolute clear. Instead of the normal shallow lagoon, it goes deep down under the city. The fact that a water body would be the deepest at the shore contradicts logic! Something here is turned upside down! Also I can see healthy forests, without a trace of human presence, along the opposite side of "the lake."*

After I awoke, it was clear to me that in the first part of the dream I had to experience the extreme alienation of our culture, alienation that is normally hidden from our eyes through self-produced illusions. I realized that the clump of our civilization is blocking the very source of Gaia's life energies and angelic inspirations, like the cork on a bottle. These Gaia-related qualities were presented to me in the second part of the dream as pristine spring water surrounding "Venice" and the virgin forest on the mainland.

Could we say that a similar unpleasant veil of alienation, presented in the dream through the image of "Venice," is also covering our body, not allowing its pristine powers and qualities to express themselves in an optimal way?

It is not my intention to deny the functional excellence of our physical bodies. Not at all! They are a masterpiece of Gaia's elemental architects. The problem is—I apologize for repeating again—the aggressive attitude of the modern human mind, covering the body with a membrane of extreme density so that the human body is not able to develop the intensity demanded by the rhythms of rapidly changing cosmic cycles.

Why is a different development needed, given that our bodies function in a relatively perfect way? It is needed because there are many dimensions of our being, explored in the previous chapters, that belong to our essence, yet can not express fully through the present body. To be able to find their proper way of expression, a body is needed that is of a more transparent nature. This would allow finer layers of our being, which are presently condemned to be invisible, to find their form of manifestation, even if not appearing in a physical way.

Are we going to lose the material quality of our body and become ghost-like beings? Not at all! Being able to exist as manifested beings of life in a material form is the great invention of Gaia appreciated by the universe. Performing the next step and freeing the body of its extreme condensation would enable new synergies between different aspects of the multidimensional reality within us, thus further perfecting the physical qualities of the body.

*The bones as the foundation of the body*

Before we begin observing the material composition of the human body, I need to remind you that the body materials we are dealing with are a certain aspect of Gaia consciousness. It appears to the human mind that stones, bones, and bodies (in general) are objects of fixed matter. It only seems so because the fantastic input of the elemental beings is ignored. For the most part unobserved, they work to permanently translate ideas created by the Gaia consciousness into corresponding compositions of material particles. As a result of this creative process, Gaia's inspirations (sometimes collaborating with human creativity) appear in front of our eyes as stones, organic phenomena, beings, buildings, and objects. Even though bones appear to our senses as hard objects, we should remember that their hardness is not hardness in itself, but simply information about a specific quality related to the bones that can be labeled "hard."

My insight says that a skeleton from the prospective of Gaia consciousness is primarily an expression of the fire element collaborating with the world of minerals. Minerals represent a kind of consciousness capable of creating conditions for different expressions of the fire element to embody.

To be practical, let me present my perceptions related to the skeleton as the foundation of the human body's construction. I am aware of three simultaneous phases through which the skeleton comes into existence.

### First phase

I perceive the skeleton in the first phase as a subtle fire element structure surrounding the body and holding it safely within the rhythms of its intersecting planes. The fire element structure has crystal-shaped forms and a sound quality. If asked the source of the wonderful crystal structure, then I would point to beams of light emanating from the core of the Earth. They direct my attention toward Gaia as the primary source. The fiery forms of the body foundation seem to evolve from sounds that are constantly emanating from the core of Gaia.

### Second phase

The first phase does not show any relationship to the actual skeleton. It is the second phase that translates the fiery and crystalline rhythms dancing around the body into the patterns of the future skeleton. The center of the perfect presence focused in the pelvic cavity takes on the role of translator in cooperation with the personal elemental being. The subtle network of the skeleton comes into existence, capable of moving in resonance with our decision about our position in the ambience, our equilibrium, and the desired movement's direction.

*Third phase*

In the third phase, the noosphere of minerals steps into the process, making possible the foundation of our body's holon to materialize as the skeleton. The input of mineral consciousness can be perceived in the form of streams of fluid minerals that adjust in each moment to the impulses issued by the first two phases. Subsequently, the minerals are capable of providing the human mind with information needed for us to believe that we have firmly materialized bones joined together into a skeleton.

The following Gaia Touch exercise can support both aspects of our personal grounding, being anchored in the core of Gaia as the source of our stability as well as in the crystal light structure woven around the body.

## The skin — the facade of the body

After attuning to the foundation of our personal building, the next area of interest is its facade, known as the skin. The skin is considered to be the largest organ of our body, performing many important functions. It holds the different extensions of our body together, bound into a whole. It is a wonderful organ of perception, a breathing organ, and a medium of communication with the environment.

Through three dreams that I received shortly one after another, I was inspired with the idea that skin is about to reveal new dimensions that until now were hidden from our perception. Better to say, they only existed as potentials.

Let me start with the first dream:

*It is early morning and I am walking toward the place where I was supposed to lead a workshop in the open landscape. Suddenly I notice that the weather is changing. While I sense cold weather approaching, I realize that I am not dressed properly. Looking at my clothing, I am deeply frightened. I am dressed in a woman's white robe, not suitable for a man. Its patterning shows a composition of big holes of spindle-shaped forms.*

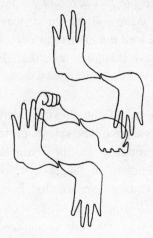

## HAND COSMOGRAM FOR GROUNDING AND ANCHORING IN THE COSMIC WHOLE

1. Position your hands in front of your belly (at a distance from the body of about ten inches). There, in the depth of the pelvic cavity, pulsates the focus responsible for your presence here and now. There is the place of our inner stability.

2. One hand faces outward with the palm open and the fingers stretched upward. The other points downward with the palm turned inward and the fingers stretched downward. Only the thumb tips of both hands are touching each other.

3. Be aware that the four fingers, pointing downward are anchoring you in the core of Gaia as the source of love that holds all beings grounded upon the Earth—usually it is called "the power of gravitation."

4. At the same time the four fingers pointing upward send rays of light high up, touching the stars to anchor you in the widths of the universe. Remain in that anchoring position for a moment.

5. Next, fold the four fingers of both hands into a fist, while the thumbs are still touching in front of your belly, to reinforce your centering in the focus responsible for your presence here and now.

6. Open your fingers again, as described above, to reinforce the anchoring in the dimensions of the Earth and the universe.

7. Continue for a while with the alternating rhythm of centering in the focus of the belly and anchoring yourself in the depths of the Earth and the widths of the universe.

*How can I stand the cold weather for the whole day dressed
like this? I plan to make a detour on my way and visit my friend
William who could lend me his winter coat. But I realize that he
is much larger in his shoulders, and that the warm coat would
not fit me.*

The final sequence of the dream underlines the difference
between the old principle of the skin as protection against influences from the environment and the new principle. The new (perhaps additional) function of the skin is seemingly ineffective,
which causes my sincere concern that it may not prevent my
freezing. But my following meditations showed that this concern
is out of place. The skin structure, symbolized by the white femi-
nine-like perforated dress, opens new understanding of our body's
facade.

Looking closely at the dress structure, I realized it has three
components. Two of them can be described as silvery and white
threads, composing the material of the dress. The third component
has the form of the spindle shaped holes, which are framed by the
weaving of the threads. Let me try to describe their function as I
perceive it.

The silvery shimmering threads of the dress symbolize a kind
of protective membrane. I can see it positioned around the body
at least 20 inches away from it. The membrane is composed of a
multitude of mandala-shaped units in constant movement. As a
consequence, it does not enclose the body like armor because it
includes free spaces that can close or open according to the need
of the moment. Even though it is of a subtle nature, I believe that
the silvery, shimmering aspect of this skin is capable of protecting
the body from radiation overdose or other harmful influences.

The white threads, of which the dress is woven, represent a
new kind of perception, made possible through a "new" layer of
the skin, as presented in the dream. It is composed of many clusters of body sensors related to different aspects of the multidimensional world. They make possible the simultaneous perception
of different layers of reality, with great clarity.

The spindle-shaped holes of the dress represent a new aspect
of the skin's breathing function. Food is being respired, not air!

Food that can be absorbed by the body through the skin has a fairy-like quality (known as honeydew or manna). This new layer of the skin allows an additional function of breathing to feed oneself. The dream also underlines that, as a man, I was dressed in feminine clothes. Symbolic language translates this to mean that the newly revealed skin dimensions create the possibility for the feminine facet of the human body to fully express. As a gift of Gaia, continually woven through the tenderness of her voice, it is already potentially present within the human skin.

## The black skin layer

The second dream made me aware of a black layer of the skin:

*I am shown a group of women moving in a row through a dark tunnel. They are dressed in shimmering black pelerines reaching down to the ground, with their heads covered with high pointed black hats. In the next image the same women wear normal clothes and are washing laundry.*

The last sequence of the dream asserts that the women appearing in the black capes do not represent some kind of magical ritual, but represent something related to everyday reality. The black capes covering the bodies of the women indicate an unrecognized, until now, aspect of the skin. Further, one can imagine the dark side of the skin as complementary to the "white" surface of the body, or as the skin's back side. One would have to dive under the surface of the skin and look at it from inside the body to perceive its black aspect.

From that prospective, the skin appears as a thin layer, or even a border, separating the outer daylight world from the inner space of the body. From inside looking out, the skin would appear as dark as the darkest night. Looking at the back side of the skin would appear like an open window, looking at the black night sky covered with a multitude of tiny stars. Relating to our conversation in the first part of the book about the causal and manifested worlds, the black skin layer would belong to the causal dimension of the skin.

*The dream about the black skin layer*

From this point of view it is possible to understand the shimmering of the black capes in the dream and the women's pointed hats. The shimmering of the capes can be compared to the mentioned "stars" visible at the inner side of the skin. Looking closer at those stars, I realize they represent tiny holes in the skin through which the daylight trickles into the inner spaces of the body. The conical caps represent these pores associated with the interdimensional portals to the surface—see the drawing in the Intermezzo II (p. 157), representing the two "conical caps" of such a portal. Such tiny pores in the skin function as the eye of a needle, through which the light of the manifested world shines into the inside realms of the body. Vice-versa, the "dark" (causal) dimension of the body leaks outward, through the same pores, into the manifested world.

The skin at this level enables the flow of exchange between the causal worlds of the body and the manifested world outside. Diving into the inner space of the body, the life powers get regenerated in their causal layers. Also regenerated are the qualities inherited from the plant, animal, and elemental worlds. In the reversed path, these qualities get translated into the rhythms of everyday life and creativity. Inhalation and exhalation function simultaneously at this level.

## The silky grey skin layer

Between the white and the black skin layer, I perceive a thin silvery grey layer, existing only at the back of the body. But the following dream asserts that it also has some influence upon the daylight world in front.

I received this dream while taking a short nap in an airplane between Rio de Janeiro and Rome:

*I realize that between the back of my white shirt and the inside of my dark colored jacket there is another piece of cloth of thin, grey, silk-like material. It covers only my back. It is tied to the front of my body with three horizontal grey ribbons. I feel confused. Aesthetics dictate that the ribbons should be at the back, not in front of the body.*

The quality of the fine silk-like material calls forth the memory of our parallel evolution with the Sidhe, of the so-called fairy world. Is it possible that, without awareness, human beings carry among our skin layers a gift received ages ago from our sister evolution?

So far, I have succeeded in identifying two functions of the silky-grey skin layer:

- It makes it possible to see the world in the way that fairy beings perceive it, to be aware of the given ambience in all its different dimensions simultaneously. One has the sensation of looking through lenses uniformly distributed upon the front of the body, into the world behind the back. You stand in the back space of the causal world and look through the lenses from there into the manifested world.
- It also enables movement through time dimensions without being bound by the rules of linear time and space. It would be as if you had a propeller on your back, capable of lifting you from the ground and positioning you at any desired point in time and space.

# 3

# THE MATERIALS COMPOSING THE HOUSE OF THE BODY

After getting to know the foundation and facade of our house, we need to enter into and experience the building materials of the house of our body. As usual, we will set aside most of the rich mental knowledge concerning body materials. We shall concentrate upon those elements that until now existed more or less unnoticed as pure potential. But in the context of the Earth transmutation process, they may become the primary carriers of our bodily existence.

## The body is primarily a water body

Gliding with intuition into my body, I experience it as a highly condensed mass of water. To make up the usual body forms, the water units are organized—better to say, held together—by fine transparent membranes, kind of subtle bags.

This perception is related to the manifested level of the body. Seen from the causal level, I perceive the human water body as a spindle-shaped form, as presented in Chapter 1, Part II, dealing with the resonances of the Pacific and Atlantic oceans within us (pp. 106 ff). The upper part of the spindle-shaped water body resonates with the Atlantic, the lower one with the Pacific.

The spindle-shaped watery space of the body is, of course, unable to stand upright, as a human being should. It can stand upright only through the existence of the fire element-based crystalline structure around the body related to the skeleton (as described in the previous chapter on the body's architecture). This is the case where the water and fire bodies collaborate.

The two conic spaces of the water body touch with their grounding circles at the solar plexus area. Here I can perceive something like the wake of a boat on the sea. This "wake," in effect, produces the horizontal channel we walked through during

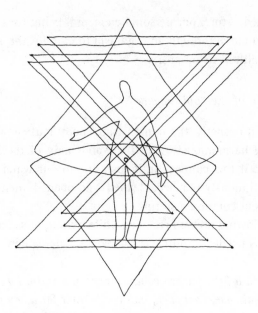

*The water body is held in place through the fire element structure*

the first part of the book. It connects the causal world positioned behind our back with the daylight world in front and vice versa.

There is a third perception of our water body. Seen from the perspective of materialized reality, the water body is compressed inside the physical body in the form of liquids, such as blood and lymph.

We are often not aware of the important function the water body plays in our life. Let me list some of its noble capacities:

- If our inner animal wants to help us understand a potentially dangerous situation, for example, its impulse would make the water body vibrate in a corresponding manner at the solar plexus. Human consciousness is capable of translating that vibration into a corresponding emotional sensation or a mental pattern.
- The water body enables the evolving of our emotional make-up. For example, it gives expression to human compassion and sympathy toward our fellow beings.
- Inspirations from the world of ancestors and descendents can be conveyed to a given person through vibrations of the water body.

- As stated before, our personal elemental being uses the water body to move through an organism to care for the well-being and health of its organs.

## Getting rid of the "old luggage"

To function properly, the human water body must be capable of resonating harmoniously with the water body of the Earth and its oceans. If this connection is lost, due to our water body not being continuously purified, cleaned, and opened, then the result is permanent emotional storms.

The following dream I received while writing this chapter hints at the steps needed to purify the personal water sphere:

*Traveling in a fully packed compartment of a train, I am forced to leave my suitcase, backpack, and coat rather far away in the corridor. It makes me nervous because my identification documents are in my backpack. We arrive unexpectedly early at the station. Jumping from my seat, I run out of the train so as not to miss my station, forgetting my coat and luggage.*

*But the train does not move forward. I ask the train conductor if I have enough time to jump in to fetch my luggage. He agrees. I jump in, but now the space inside the train has transformed from long and rectangular to circular. I am amazed at the new form of the space. The luggage does not seem to be important any more.*

Sitting in the train symbolizes taking part in the present linear form of space and time. On returning to the train, I was made aware of the epochal change now coming into being. The linear space and time structure changes into the new circular form of the nine-dimensional Earthly Cosmos. In the course of change, some aspects of human "luggage," symbolized by the coat, the suitcase, and the backpack, have lost their importance. Asking myself what could be symbolized by the redundant luggage I decided upon the following:

- The coat represents different roles we play in our life, or from our past.

- The suitcase stands for the collective traumas of the human race that we carry in our personal noosphere.
- The backpack, with identity documents, symbolizes false concepts concerning our identity that we produce or are projected upon us in the course of our lives. We carry them around perhaps so as not to lose our formal status in society.

We are at the threshold of apocalyptic dimensional changes. Human beings should detach from this "old luggage," transmute its patterns, and send its clean neutralized energy back into Gaia's reservoir of primeval powers.

I have already proposed Gaia Touch exercises that can be of help in the great cleansing process—the Healing Tear of Grace, for example. The exercise on the following page was recommended to me in a dream. I was made aware that the angelic network of Gaia has installed a kind of "Halls of Transmutation" in the causal world to help clean the planet. Worn-out patterns and energy clusters can be directed there for recycling with the help of the violet micro-portals shown in the exercise.

## The sacred functions of blood

Blood comes into being when the dragon powers of Gaia mate with a specific cosmic inspiration of Sophia. The fire of the Earth has to meet the Cosmic fire in the ambience of the water element. What emerges from the union is a permanent stream of life circulating between the cosmic and the earthly dimensions.

I perceive the stream of life within the veins and arteries as the mythical "thread of life." It can be seen as circulating within the blood stream as a thin red thread, woven from primeval (dragon) powers. It represents the essence of life existing behind the physical blood. It is impossible to express in words how unique and precious the thread of life is. Those who are present at the death of a loved one, at the moment when the thread of life is cut off by the decree of the Black Goddess, understand to treasure its sacredness.

I was shown the source of this life thread by my personal elemental being. He took me to the perfect presence in the depth of the belly. There I was introduced to the mighty angels of Gaia

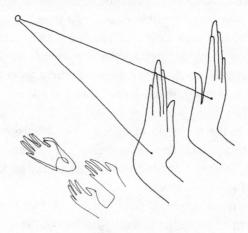

Gaia Touch exercise of transmutation

1. All problematic patterns of behavior or false images of identity have their anchor in the causal back space. Choose the one you would like to transmute.

2. Imagine it hanging in your back space in the form of a symbol or other image. If needed, support the image with the accompanying emotional patterns.

3. Then reach with your hands into the back space and bring the given visual/emotional pattern through your body into your front space.

4. If needed, you can now perform the gesture of detachment, to get energetically free from its bonds. Hold your hands horizontally in front of your body, powerfully squeezed together, having the purpose of the detachment in your mind. Then pull your hands apart with the optimum power to annihilate the given attachment. (See the drawing on the left.)

5. Imagine in front of you a glowing violet dot positioned in the far distance, representing the portal leading to the Halls of Transmutation.

6. Push the pattern or energy involved with the corresponding gesture toward the violet portal, imagining that it gets smaller and smaller till it disappears within the violet dot.

7. While pushing, the hands get closer and closer to each other to the point of overlapping.

8. The transmuting process is completed. Give thanks!

responsible for the thread of life moving from being to being, from one sequence of life to another. I could feel their giant light bodies in constant rhythmical movement. Their rhythm is echoed by the beating of the heart.

The question arose in me of what kind of cosmic inspiration is involved in making blood such a sacred substance. In answer to my question, I was led into the space of the heart where I was shown the holographic presence of a being that could be called the "Angel of Freedom." What does the cosmic quality of freedom have to do with the stream of blood? It is true that heroic myths often praise those who sacrificed their blood for the freedom of their homeland. But this may be only a glimpse of what blood means in relation to the quality of freedom.

Entering into communion with the Angel of Freedom, I realized how immensely fortunate we are as embodied beings. Our thread of life is incarnated. As a consequence we are blessed with an infinite number of possibilities to touch, to move, and to create. We are free to embrace each other and to make love. It may seem normal to us. But it is just the opposite! It is a cosmic gift of unprecedented value that we share with the animals. All other beings of the universe envy us human beings who are embodied with blood penetrating our muscles and consequently triggering their movements. Following the streams of blood within my body I felt as if moving within the temple of freedom, with pockets full of gold.

What a shame that human beings have forgotten the potential of cosmic freedom carried within our blood. We allow adverse forces to bind us to all kinds of addictions and slaveries! We are not aware that in the stream of our blood we carry one of the precious gifts offered by the divinity, the freedom to dance through life as an embodied being.

Blood is not a neutral substance, nor is it our private property. The blood in our bodies is a manifestation of the divine will to embody the universe as a community of living and loving beings.

## *The threat of losing the thread of life*

After becoming aware of how precious the Thread of Life is that we share with the animal kingdom, I received a dream as a warning that we may all lose this unique gift if humans continue to be ignorant of its meaning for us, for animals, and for the universe as the whole:

*Together with a group of men we are binding beautiful healthy horses to be burned four by four. Each of the four horses is to be bound over an opening in the floor from which deadly flames will rise to turn them instantly to ash. Taking it as something absolutely normal, we are about to bind the first four horses to be burned.*

*I am astonished that the threads that we use to bind them are so thin and delicate. They are the color of blood. I say to myself, this is crazy; these strong horses will tear their binds to pieces and escape death when the gas burners under the floor are ignited. Thick iron chains should be used instead.*

It took me a while to understand that we were binding the horses with the strongest material that has ever existed; the thread of life!

The warning of the dream is that the thread of life is something more then the life force that flows within the blood of human and animal bodies. It is the precondition for existence in general. Attuning to the thread of life beyond its incarnation within the streams of blood, I perceive gigantic waterfalls distributed throughout the universe. Positioned at different levels of space, they represent thresholds with enormous masses of water rushing from one level to another—water, representing in this image the power to be—the will to exist.

Through cool-headed killing of our fellow animals and human beings, not only is the free flow of the life force threatened, but also the very existence of the universe as the home of innumerable beings embodied at different levels of existence.

Inspired by the soul of Venice, I created the following Gaia Touch exercise, which I consider an expression of our will to hold the Thread of Life unbroken. The hands are at first positioned— seen from the side—in the form of the Grand Canal of Venice. The Grand Canal is polarized so that the part from Santa Lucia (the area of the railway station) to the Rialto Bridge is of earthly

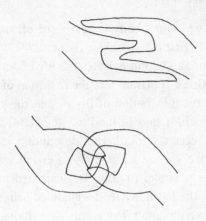

VENETIAN GAIA TOUCH EXERCISE TO HOLD SAFE THE
THREAD OF LIFE

1. Position both hands in front of your heart space so that
   the four fingers above and the fingers of the other hand
   below are positioned horizontally. Both thumbs reach into
   the space in between.
2. Feel the quality of water pulsating between your hands.
3. Turn one hand 90 degrees to the left, and the other simultaneously 90 degrees to the right.
4. In the next moment, join both thumbs with the respective
   forefingers in the form of two rings that reach into one
   another.
5. Repeat the exercise several times in succession. If you wish
   to relate to a specific place or situation where the thread of
   life is endangered, then you should combine the gesture with
   visualizing a corresponding symbol or image.

nature. From there to its mouth at San Marco it shows cosmic
characteristics. It can be seen as a symbol of the Thread of Life
holding both poles united. For this reason the Canal Grande had,
up to modern times, only one bridge—the Rialto—to symbolize
the marriage between the two poles as the basis of life.

No less important is the quality of water that enables the
Thread of Life to manifest. Canal Grande can be seen as a sanctuary of the water element.

*What about muscles?*

If asked what the human body is composed of, the logical mind would emphasize first our muscular tissue.

The Gospel of Saint John narrates the life of Jesus of Nazareth (later called in Greek "Christos"). In the first lines of the first chapter it pinpoints the incarnation of Divinity as the greatest cosmic event of our epoch. It says in the Prologue (1:14) that the divine creative word became "flesh." This description is not accurate. It should say that we are witnessing an epoch when something unique becomes possible: Divinity is incarnated into the human body and walks the Earth inside an embodied being!

This is my interpretation. The words, "the divine creative word became flesh," tells us how important a step it is in the evolution of the universe. This is the embodiment of the lofty light-woven worlds into the muscular tissue of the body, be it human or animal in origin. But it would be a sacrilege to consider the rational/physical level only. The muscular tissue of the human body is permeated and moved by the blood stream, incorporating the inherent cosmic Thread of Life. Only then the divine Essence finds the conditions to incarnate.

This is displayed in the famous Renaissance frescoes created in the Sistine Chapel in Rome by Michelangelo Buonarotti. Christos, the central figure in the fresco of the Last Judgment, is painted as a classic Greek athlete. Church authorities heavily criticized Michelangelo for the nakedness of the Christos body and other figures of the saints, and Michelangelo's own assistants were hired to paint clothing on the figures.

What a shame! I believe that Michelangelo took the words of the Gospel in earnest, considering the body manifested "in flesh" to be equal to Divinity embodied—not thinking only about the body of Jesus of Nazareth!

We are fortunate that in the Urban Bibliotheca of Lucca, Italy, a miniature is preserved from the book written by abbess Hildegard von Bingen, *Liber Divinorum Operum*, that relates to the divine nature of the incarnated human body. The illustration called "The Cosmic Human Being" was painted around the year 1240. The vision of the abbess shows many similarities to our theory.

*Hildegard von Bingen's vision of the integral human being*

Let us start with the center of the image:

- At the center of the cosmos stands the human being "in flesh"—which means with distinctive muscular tissue.
- The center of the human being is shown with a brownish red sphere around its hips, pinpointing "the focus of the perfect presence" (see pp. 172-173).
- The human body is surrounded by three qualities of water that can be identified as: the general body of water related to the oceans, the water of the emotional aura, and the sacred aspect called the Water of Life.
- The water body is surrounded with, and held together in its totality, by the red Thread of Life.
- The Gaia-related origin of the Thread of Life is connected with many different animals that pop out of the red thread. They are also drinking from the water of the oceans that we share with the animal kingdom.

- The Sophia-related origin of the Thread of Life is presented by the red hands of Sophia embracing the thread.
- Sophia has a double head. The upper head one can easily identify with her masculine aspect, the Christ. Sophia's head is wholly red (except the eyes), while Christ's head is painted with realistic features to symbolize his embodiment in flesh.
- The head above the human being, with four golden chakras above, sending two golden rays over the human figure, can be identified as the head of Gaia.

## The role of the fire body

When copying the miniature featuring the vision of Hildegard von Bingen, I noticed that there are many golden rays spread over the original. Some of them emanate from tiny stars woven into the Thread of Life. Others emerge from the mouths of different animals. I believe that they represent the crystal light structure discussed in the previous chapter. We got to know it as the foundations upon which the house of our body is built.

Indeed; even if the water body as presented at the beginning of this chapter is of basic importance for our body's vitality, there must be an agent that moves the life force throughout the body. What else could act complementary to the water masses but the fire element?

Fire does not appear only in the form of flames but is also equal to light as representing one of the four basic aspects of the cosmic consciousness. Encountered in the manifested world, we know the elements as water, fire, earth, and air.

The element of fire can be considered as the oldest of the four elements. Let me list some of its characteristics:
- Fire is the carrier of joy and inspiration. Muses, as highly evolved elemental beings and the source of creative inspirations, are beings of the fire element.
- Fire is sensitive to the changes of cosmic cycles, and as such it becomes an agent of transformation. When cycles change, the destructive aspect of fire bursts forth, decomposing what is obsolete. On the other hand, it acts as a supporter of inspiration for new developments.

- Fire does not know anything but the present moment. As a consequence, history, the common timeline of our world, is alien to the Fire element. The Fire element supports the essence, and only the essence, of everything, our body including.
- The element of Fire stands for the sacred dimension of reality. If the fire is allowed to pulsate freely between the causal and manifested dimensions of the world, then the sacredness of everyday life is secured.
- Being woven into the Thread of Life, fire marks the beginning and the end of life. The inspiration to give birth to a living being and cutting the Thread of Life at the moment of death are both acts of the Fire element.

While fire performs a key role in life, the misuse of the divine powers of the Fire element for killing and for religious entanglement has caused substantial damage to the sacred dimension of the human fire body. Instead of permeating the whole being, its sacred dimension is pushed into the back space, depriving it of its capacity to serve as a source of blessing for daily life.

To experience the quality of inspiration carried by the Fire element I propose the Peace Meditation on the following page. Peace inspirations are carried by muses (as mentioned above).

The white dove of peace was born representing the human's will to embody peace on Earth. But without an olive branch in its beak, the archetypal powers of Gaia, giving peace the strength to manifest in life and political situations, are missing. Without the cooperation of the loving dragon powers of Gaia, symbolized by the strength and nourishing power of the olive tree, there is no hope for a lasting peace.

## Changes concerning body materials

Returning to the miniature of Hildegard von Bingen featuring the integral human being, I would point out that animals are depicted to be holding in their mouths most of the golden threads that help the human being appear in its proper form. They symbolize the crystal light structure woven around the human body, functioning as body's foundation.

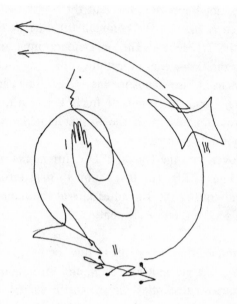

PEACE MEDITATION WITH THE DOVE, THE OLIVE BRANCH,
AND THE MUSE OF PEACE

1. Enter your inner peace. Then call the idea of peace forth
   from your heart space with the prayer gesture.

2. Lead the white dove from your heart space through your
   throat in a downward bow toward the deepest point of your
   pelvic cavity. There, upon the pubic bone, an olive branch
   is positioned.

3. Along its flight downward the dove picks up the olive
   branch. Some moments may be needed here to feel the quality embodied by the olive tree.

4. Continuing its circular flight toward your back space, the
   dove with the olive branch then arrives at the point behind
   your heart. There the third element of peace needs to be
   integrated.

5. The point behind your heart is the focus of the muse of peace.
   She stands for the peace quality. Give yourself enough time
   to experience the quality of her inspiration.

6. Afterward, the dove of peace continues its flight above your
   head toward the manifested world, distributing the inspiration for peace worldwide.

Hildegard's vision shows us that in the present epoch of the body's development, animal archetypes play a substantial role in upholding the human fire body. Obviously a great part of our fire body is inherited from our animal ancestors.

Is it possible that this kind of relationship between the animal kingdom and the human body has changed recently? In the Intermezzo I we talked about the animals' desire to retrieve form from the human body, to reconnect with their archetypes. They do not wish to serve us humans as slaves anymore, carrying us piggyback, as little children are carried.

This will lead to a fundamental change in our body structure, the extent of which can be intuited in the following dream:

*I am very amazed at the realization that what I previously knew as veins for the transportation of body liquids are now made of raw wood. However, these are not dead tree trunks, hollowed out to serve as channels, but are channels made of plant substance belonging to living tree trunks. I am also shown vessels for holding water that resemble different body organs made of wooden material.*

The living tree trunks represent the plant kingdom, as a complementary to the animal world. Are plants taking over the role that animals want to be free of? Meditating upon the message of the dream, I realized that the plant kingdom is not about to substitute for animals in their role of holding the human body in its proper inner and outer forms. This would make no real change. Only the servants would be exchanged.

The real change in the constitution of the body that was conveyed in the dream has to do with the plant aspect within us being ready to become more active in the role of helping us incarnate in the physical body. As a consequence, the proper balance between our animal and plant supporters would be established.

This could be a proper step for human beings to become more responsible for the exceptional gift of our organic (material) body. We have to learn (with the help of the personal elemental being) to be anchored within the primary sources of life and not to expect that somebody else will do it for us. Plants could be our teachers. They could teach us how to exist as embodied beings by grounding ourselves in the primeval powers of Gaia, continually transforming these powers into our body functions in every moment.

The decision of a growing number of people to follow a vegetarian way of life is a sign that the change is on course.

In another dream I was shown the body meridians composed of two parts like a zipper. If the zipper opens, then we get two autonomous parts of the meridian. Imagine one half staying in place and the other connecting with different points in the environment.

The body meridians are considered to be the transporters of life energy. They make the circulation of life energy through the body possible. Splitting the meridian into two parts causes the unexpected to happen. The life force does not circulate only within the body but also between the body and its environment. When attuning to such functioning of the meridians, I feel almost weightless. I move through life easily and joyfully. I believe that this way human being could walk upon water.

Also, in this case of collaboration between the human being and its natural ambience, I see the prospect for the further development of the body.

The following Gaia Touch exercise can convey the experience of recreating the body structure. It is a gift of Siena, an ancient town in Italy. In my workshop there I discovered that Siena knows the secret of how to co-create the world of form from Gaia's archetypal life powers.

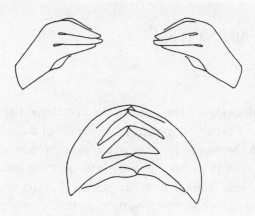

GAIA TOUCH EXERCISE TO STIMULATE THE RE-CREATION
OF THE EMBODIED WORLD STRUCTURE

1. The hands are positioned on both sides of the body at the
   level of the solar plexus.

2. Press the fingers of both hands into one point to symbolize
   the concentration of the primeval powers of creation.

3. Then lead both hands toward each other, while the fingers
   become more and more open.

4. When both hands meet in front of the solar plexus, both sets
   of the five fingers are open to their full extent.

5. In that moment, the tips of the fingers meet. You can imagine their meeting as two cymbals bumping one into another.
   The gesture symbolizes your will to awaken to your individual role in the body's (or world's) self-creating process.

6. The inaudible sound thus produced is equal to the "big bang"
   at the moment of creation. It did not happen only once in the
   past, of course, but repeats at each moment anew.

7. Repeat the exercise a few times with a short pause between
   each sequence. Then listen to the changes within.

# 4

# THE HEART SYSTEM

Walking through the body during the first three chapters of Part III, dear co-traveler, we gathered experiences of those aspects that concern the human body as the whole. Now the moment has come when we need to gather the courage to enter the inner spaces of certain organs. With the term "inner spaces" I refer to their causal dimensions. To enable this journey, in the Intermezzo II a key was given to us in the form of the 12-dimensional world model. We shall not deal with the manifested dimensions (looking at the organs from the outside, with the rational mind). We shall instead walk through the organs, relating to their causal dimensions.

*The superficial projections blocking the heart system*

In human awareness—certainly in Western culture—the heart is adorned with an uplifted meaning. To make something sound precious we say it comes "from the heart." Is it possible that the over-evaluation of the heart is a mental trick to hide from humanity the exquisite qualities and powers of the heart, so that they can not express fully and in a grounded way in our culture and everyday situations? Indeed, a culture that proclaims the superiority of the heart should not be as destructive as ours is.

Another problematic conception is that the loving quality of the heart should be able to balance the aggressive attitude of the mind, which governs the modern world. It is true that the loving nature of the heart can provide the proper balance to the dry mind. But such an approach causes another imbalance, concentrating the whole dynamics of consciousness into the upper part of the body. As a result it is easy to ignore the treasures of the pelvic cavity, and especially the presence of Gaia at the point of the perfect presence. And so, the powers of the heart lose their grounding, becoming ineffective in one of their basic functions: the generation of peace and mutual understanding among peoples of the Earth.

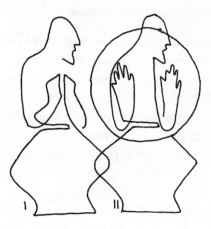

*Santiago di Compostela gesture of opening the heart*

To have a personal experience of the authentic quality of the heart system I propose the following Gaia Touch exercise. The inspiration came to me after arriving at the goal of the pilgrimage route to Santiago di Compostela. I was prompted to look at the representation carved on the medieval portal of the cathedral, where the Christ can be seen with a heart-opening gesture

GAIA TOUCH EXERCISE TO EXPERIENCE THE AUTHENTIC
QUALITY OF THE HEART SYSTEM

1. Hold your hands upward in front of your heart center, forming a praying gesture.

2. When you are ready, start opening your hands very slowly, like a door opening.

3. Continue opening until the backs of your hands are at your chest and you can open no further. Continue the opening of the door in your imagination, until the sides of your gate are swung open completely at the back.

4. Now is the moment to enter the space of your heart from the back and gather experiences of its true essence. The back side of the heart realm is the proper entrance.

5. Returning to the initial prayer gesture and closing the door finishes the exercise. This counts as a thanksgiving.

## The constellation of the heart centers

Entering the region of the heart in front of the chest and looking around, I get the feeling of floating in the middle of a "solar system." A "sun" is shining at the center of the wide space, encircled by a number of "planets" positioned at different distances from it. The space of this solar system seems to be wider then the human thorax, expanding beyond its limits.

First I wish to ponder about the meaning of these planets—later a chapter will be dedicated to this sun around which the planets are circling. Each one of them appears to me as a jewel in itself, different in color, form, and quality. I understand them as different focuses of love generated by the heart system. They represent different doors through which human beings communicate with the manifested worlds of nature and culture—and with their fellow beings at different levels of existence.

I wish first to present my perception of some of the planets of the heart system, although, not being yet able to explain from where their powers and qualities originate, this list might not be complete:

### The focus of heartfelt connections
I perceive it as a tiny red angular stone. In its capacity as a heart center it enables the human being to come into a loving relationship with any of the innumerable beings belonging to the family of life extending throughout the Earthly Cosmos.

### The focus of freedom
I can see it in the form of a rounded green "pea." Its potential enables us to express the freedom of the heart; the power of joy that does not know any borders.

### The focus of family love
I perceive it as a tiny white ball radiating from inside to outside. Its quality encompasses partner love in the broadest sense of the word, including loving relationships in a family and in the field of partnership in creative work or common dedication to certain goals.

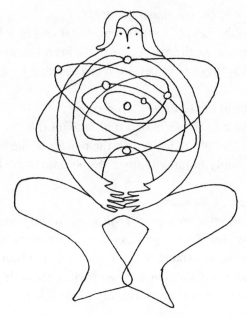

*The constellation of the heart centers*

*A holographic piece of the fairy heart*

It does not have any form. It appears in the space of the human heart system, each moment new, like a comet upon the night sky. We humans could learn from it that love is real only in the given moment, and therefore needs each successive moment be awakened anew.

*A holographic piece of Gaia's love*

I can see it as a tiny golden ball with a white ring around it. Its capacity is to translate the power of love into any aspect of existence or creativity. If I attune to it, then I become aware of my capacity as a human being to become the pure presence of love in the world.

*The power of the heart to manifest*

It represents the power of the heart to translate infinity into time structures, and etheric space into manifested reality. I perceive it in the form of the eye of a needle. The eye of a needle symbolizes the portal leading from one dimension to another.

### The focus of the emotional quality

I see it in the form of a shimmering water crystal. It has the ability to transform the diverse powers of the heart into emotional impulses, so that they can be perceived and absorbed by other beings.

### The focus of the heart and mind synergy

I perceive it in the form of a tiny brilliant star. Its ability is to imbue the ideas of the mind with the powers of the heart, which means the ability to think through the wisdom of the heart.

### The crown of the heart

I first noticed it as a pearl positioned in the hollow between the two clavicles. Such a position at the base of the throat has a symbolic meaning related to the capacity of the heart to inspire human creativity. Its presence shows itself to me in the form of an intense blue color that permeates my whole being.

## Grounding the heart system

I was warned in a dream that my perceptions of the human heart constellation might be too shallow if I did not investigate the problem that can make the heart system float ungrounded.

*I am the observer of a group of beautiful fairy-like women, who are dressed in fine veils, moving cheerfully over a field. While moving, they seem not to touch the ground at all. I know that they represent different qualities anchored within the human heart space. They are even called by names, but I cannot remember them.*

*Then a severe voice says that the dog is not allowed to join the group. Indeed I see a strong brown dog sitting at the side of the scene, who is being prevented from moving from there.*

Tuning to the group of the fairy-like women, I find myself in the ambience of the heart. Each of them represents one of the centers of the heart space, listed above. But what is the role of the dog? In answer to my question, the dog from the dream enters my pelvic cavity and curls up at the center of the perfect presence, as if he has found a suitable place to rest.

In one of the very first chapters of this book, while addressing our relationship to the animal world, animals were praised as ancestors of the human heart. Consequently, one should be attentive if the animal in my dream makes me aware that the exquisite heart system cannot blossom to its full potentials if it is not linked with the pelvic cavity. The heart system can vibrate in resonance with the core of Gaia only if it is connected to the point of the perfect presence at its center.

I now propose a Gaia Touch exercise taught to me years ago by a fairy being of an olive grove in the Adriatic region. Its purpose is to align the heart center with the focus of the perfect presence in the pelvic cavity—Gaia's presence within our body.

GAIA TOUCH EXERCISE TO
GROUND THE HEART SYSTEM
IN THE PELVIC CAVITY

1. Hold both hands below the heart center, positioned horizontally and back to back.

2. Imagine that your heart system is concentrated in the form of a sphere, which is positioned upon the palm of the upper hand.

3. Slowly lower both hands, still carrying the sphere, till you arrive at the lowest part of your belly.

4. Let the sphere of the heart system stay there for a while to connect to the point of the perfect presence and to become grounded.

5. Stay with the lower hand at that place while you raise the upper hand till the sphere with the heart system is back to its place.

6. Listen to the energy field that comes into being between your two hands.

7. Then you should open the sphere at your chest with the help of a corresponding gesture and feel the quality of the grounded heart.

## The elemental heart

How far have we come in exploring our heart system? On the one hand, we have observed the system of the different heart centers focused in front of the human chest. On the other hand, we have become aware of the focus of the perfect presence in the pelvic cavity where the heart system is grounded. Thus we have gotten to know two different levels in the body upon which the system rests. As the above exercise demonstrates, there must be a way to connect them.

The point of connection is called "the elemental heart." Looking at the human body I see the elemental heart positioned at the end of the breastbone. It represents a holographic piece (a fractal) of the heart of Gaia. Referring to the body of the planet, the heart system of Gaia exists under the Earth's surface as a network consisting of innumerable power centers that stand in resonance with each other and with the divine core of Gaia.

The personal elemental being uses the potentials of the elemental heart to hold upright the human heart system. This means that in each successive moment (attuned to the heart of the Earth) the elemental being creates energetic conditions in which our complex heart system can appear in its complexity.

One night a few days ago it was demonstrated to me how it feels if the potentials of the elemental heart are turned off. Awaking in the middle of the night, I felt myself as an empty shell. I could not feel anything, nor could I connect to anything. Just the material world deprived of life energy still existed. It took me hours to rebuild my heart system with the help of the personal elemental being.

## Water makes the space of the heart alive

There is another precondition in order that the exquisite human heart system can reveal all its potentials. It has to do with the element of water.

Modern exploration of the causal background of water — such as the photography of water crystals — made us aware that without water there is no possibility that any form of life could manifest. Water is able to receive and embody the subtle patterns of creative ideas that represent the foundation upon which all the different layers of the manifested world can be built up. The same relates to the heart system. If there is no moist atmosphere within the space occupied by the heart system, its units cannot manifest and perform their role in the life of an individual.

As presented in the first part of the book, the two great oceans, the Pacific and the Atlantic, find their resonance in the human water body; the Pacific permeating the lower and the Atlantic the upper part of the body. Just as the oceans are in constant movement because of the water streams, also the human water masses would deteriorate without any dynamics. At this point the heart muscle finds its important role within the human heart system.

Entering into the inner space of the heart muscle, what do I feel?

I feel the heart muscle to be a conscious being distributed throughout the whole body. I see it as representing the parent star of the human heart system. If one compares the described constellation of the heart centers to the solar system, then the heart muscle represents its parent star. As mentioned in the chapter on animals, the "parent star," in effect, connects the human heart system to its ancestor, the animal heart.

Taking a step further over the threshold into the causal world of the heart muscle, I realize that while moving blood along the veins, the heart also keeps the mass of the human water body in constant movement. The water stream departing from the bodily Pacific moves along the back of the body upward till the top of the head is reached. From there it falls like a waterfall through the front side of the body. The waterfall is composed of tiny and extremely subtle drops. By this, a beautiful watery ambience is created in front of the chest within which the above listed heart centers can be manifested

The waters of the bodily Atlantic, which are concentrated in the upper part of the body, take an opposite course. I see them moving backward into the region behind the heart center. From there I feel a strong push, bringing them forward to support the distribution of the heart qualities toward the manifested world in front of the body.

### The back side of the heart system

The part of the human water body in resonance with the Pacific Ocean creates the conditions in which the constellation of the heart centers in front of the chest can manifest. If I follow the movement of the Atlantic stream toward the back side of the chest I realize that there exists another set of heart centers. Does the heart system also have a back side?

From my explorations of the heart systems in certain landscapes, their composition often resembles the symbol of infinity, the lemniscate. Relating to the human body, the front loop of the lemniscate encompasses the "planets" listed before, the backside refers to another constellation of the heart centers. They embody different archetypal qualities. The role of the heart's back centers is to supply the human heart system with the qualities needed to enable love to be the most powerful creator in the Earthly Cosmos.

What is usually called "the heart chakra" appears at the point where the two loops of the lemniscate cross. This represents an interdimensional portal that enables communication between the heart centers operating in the manifested world and those kept carefully at the back. Through the portal of the "heart chakra," the qualities of the heart's causal world shine into the space in front of the body. This is the reason why the heart chakra is considered to be the source of all the heart qualities. As such, it is highly respected by different spiritual schools—but in fact it is only the portal that leads to the treasury of the heart.

What are the treasured qualities of the back space of the heart system? If the heart centers at the front side are represented as planets moving around the interdimensional portal of the "heart chakra," the focuses at the back can be compared with different stars shining in the background of the solar system. They embody certain archetypes acting as sources of inspiration for the heart system to be able to bring its blessings into the manifested world. Here is my (certainly not complete) list of the focuses belonging to the back space of the heart system:

### The star of truth

It radiates with the capability of the heart to see the truth and to distinguish the truth from illusions.

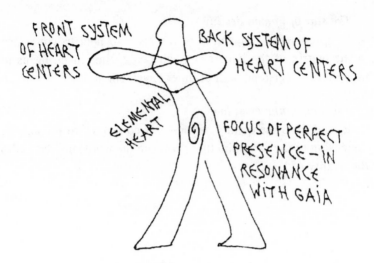

*The heart space comes into being through the interaction between the powers of the pelvic cavity and the lemniscate of the heart centers. The elemental heart is the center.*

### The compass star

It stands for the ability of the heart to act as a compass, at each moment offering the proper orientation upon the path of life. This is possible because the heart cultivates connection to divine wisdom. Divine wisdom knows the essence of the whole and the role of each particle within its totality.

### The star of inspiration

It is the source of the capability of the heart to receive divine inspirations and perceive primordial patterns needed to make creative ideas blossom.

### The star of life force

It stands for the capability of the heart to hold the dance of one's life in constant movement and transformation.

### The star of communication

It stands for the capacity of the heart to hold open the door of communication either with the personal elemental master, with the angelic world, or with the ancestors of the human race.

### The star of human destiny

It represents the capability of the heart to hold us connected to the matrix of the integral human being, thus inspiring us to proceed on a personal path of inner development.

### The star of universal love

It represents the quality of the heart connected to the angelic dimension of the Seraphim that permeate the whole universe with the quality of love.

# 5

# THE CREATIVE SCALE OF THE BODY ORGANS

## The symmetrical composition of organs

Lungs, ovaries, kidneys, vocal cords, and some of our organs of perception show the obvious pattern of pairs. We should not overlook that they are all positioned in a symmetric way along the central axis of the body.

In attempting to perceive the purpose of this symmetrical ladder of organs, I suddenly felt like a plant growing from a deep layer of soil, with five pairs of leaves arranged symmetrically along my stem. Starting from the bottom of the belly I could identify five organs corresponding to the five pairs of leaves: ovaries/testicles, liver/pancreas, kidneys, lungs, vocal cords, and eyes/ears/nostrils as a triple pair.

The experience lead me back to our exploration of the plant body of the human being and its vertical stem that we undertook in Chapter 3 in the first part of our journey. We discovered then that the stem of the archetypal plant within us can be perceived as the central axis around which the composition of the body is arranged. Further, we identified five levels of the plant within the body, which through the arrangement of the leaves show the symmetry characteristic for the plant kingdom.

At that stage of our journey we looked at the human being from outside. Now, exploring the inner spaces of the body and moving along the symmetrically arranged organs, I realize that their composition is not a static one. The pairs of organs connect in the form of a vortex dancing along the vertical "stem." Its binary rhythm comes into being through the polarized pairs of organs.

## The vortex of polarized organs

Looking more exactly at the movement of the vortex, I realized that the upward movement comes to a standstill when it reaches

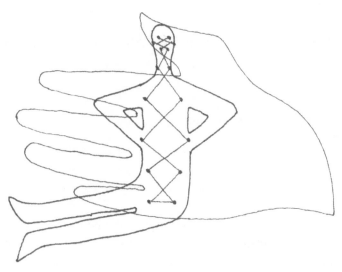

*The double vortex of body organs*

the level of the throat. The movement created by the polarized organs of perception positioned on the head (including the vocal cords) move in the opposite direction. Both movements meet in the space of the throat.

The throat is considered to be the origin of human creativity, based upon the capability of the vocal cords to transform thought patterns into words. Yet the power of the word to create does not derive from the vocal cords themselves. They are rather tools of creation—wonderful and very exact tools.

The creative power of the throat is an expression of the creative hand of Gaia working through the human body as a whole. The four pairs of organs related to the ascending vortex correspond to the four elements—the four fingers of Gaia's creative hand. They are listed below so that their alignment corresponds to the four steps of the creative process:

- The pair of lungs corresponds to the small finger (the element of air) with the ability to imbue ideas on their path toward embodiment with their autonomous consciousness.
- The pair of kidneys is related to Gaia's index finger (the element of water) with the task to provide ideas with life energy on their path toward manifestation.

- The pair of liver/pancreas relates to the middle finger (the element of fire) with the ability to transform ideas on their path toward manifestation into patterns that represent models for their future embodiment.
- The pair of ovaries/testicles corresponds to the ring finger (the element of earth) with the capacity to provide creative ideas with the possibility of embodiment in the world of form.

Yet the creative process in the name of Gaia does not work—as has been stressed a few times before—if the thumb, representing the fifth element, is not included.

In the case of the creative capacities of the human throat, the thumb of Gaia is represented by the three pairs of perception organs; the nostrils, the eyes and the ears, plus the vocal cords. If a human being is deprived of conscious perception there can be no creative process. If the activity of the vocal cords is not involved, there can be no fusion with the uprising vortex of the creative process.

The creative process, in which the binary scale of body organs is involved, has two directions of movement. The impulses of those organs that correspond to the four elements are conceived in the uprising movement, while those related to the head and the throat descend. The multidimensional space of the heart is the region of their interaction and synthesis. The region of the heart is the sacred space where human creativity can find perfectly balanced expression.

Through the creative scale of the body organs and the throat we have our capability to create with the whole body. When acting in such a way, our creation is in attuned with the creative hand of Gaia.

One should also not forget about the role of the dragon powers in the creative process (see pp. 115-127). And as well, we should not forget about the crucial role of the personal elemental master (see pp. 174-177). Without its consciousness taking care of body processes, the body organs could not interact to initiate the vortex of creative power.

To conclude I propose a Gaia Touch exercise that was conveyed to me in Humpolec, Bohemia, by the elemental guardian of the landscape called Bohemian Forest. This exercise touches upon

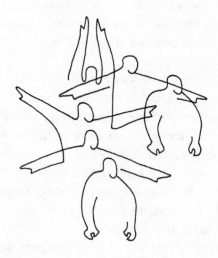

Humpolec Exercise for balancing the matter of the Earth and the light of the Universe

1. Hold your arms stretched downward, lightly held to your body. Imagine that you are concentrating the quality of the material Earth by clenching your fists strongly. Repeat this three times, like you are pumping the quality of matter into your body.

2. Then lift your arms outstretched slowly by your sides forming a large circle. Your hands are now open and the palms are directed outward. Lift your arms high until they are parallel to each other over your head to form a channel. Your palms are still directed to the outside with your arms extended parallel to each other.

3. Imagine for a moment, that the cosmic light from the widths of the universe is flowing through this channel into your body.

4. Now move your outstretched arms slowly down in such a way that you form a circle around your body. Along with this movement the earthly and the cosmic forces are being melted into unity.

5. In this way you come back to the first position and then start anew. Repeat the exercise a few times.

6. Afterward rest in silence and be aware of what is going on inside your body.

the whole spectrum of creation from dense matter to lofty cosmic realms, emphasizing the vertical channel of communication between Earth and the universe.

Be sure to give special attention to the wide circle made by the hands, which transforms the hierarchical notion of the axis.

# 6

# THE MYSTERY OF THE HEAD

Moving through the inner spaces of the body, dear co-traveler, we approach its apex—the head.

When introduced to the personal elemental being, we were lead to the grand temple of the body positioned in the pelvic cavity, the stronghold of the primary powers of Gaia. Later we moved to the next sacred cavity, the chest, with the precious system of the heart. The last, narrowest, and perhaps the least known cavity now awaits our visit—the cavity of the skull. Where is the proper door to enter the cavity of the head, to avoid falling under the influence of preconceived ideas of its identity?

*The all-prevailing presence of the head in the body*

Modern age human beings look upon the head as the greatest treasure of the body. But according to my perception there is only a small part of the treasure to be found there. What makes the human head truly a valuable piece of Gaia's creation is its distribution throughout the whole body.

When speaking about the all-prevailing presence of the head in the body, I do not think of the brain sitting in the warm ambience of the skull, of course. I think of the head as a symbol for consciousness.

Consciousness is an immensely vast cloud! We mentioned already the noosphere as the all-connected consciousness of the Earthly Cosmos. It has innumerable focuses within all beings and elements of creation, but can never be divided or even trapped in the prison of the skull. Instead, when speaking of the human aspect of consciousness, the whole body should be recognized as its original home.

Classical anatomy sees the body functioning through a network of nerve fibers. From this point of view, the brain is a computer, sending commands to control all the functions of the body through a highway of fibrous cables in the backbone. Such a mechanical understanding of the nervous system is insufficient if we want to experience the body as a seat of the noosphere—the holistic consciousness. To be successful in our search, we need to find another key that can help us understand the multidimensional nature of the human consciousness distributed throughout the body.

## The body's three-head consciousness

I know of a key that can open the door to the body as home of a richly structured sphere of consciousness. I call it "the three eyes of the Goddess." An eye, in this case, represents a specific focus of consciousness. According to the threefold principle of the Goddess, elaborated upon in the chapter "Sophia—the Divine Feminine" (see pp. 130-131), the human consciousness knows three "heads," meaning three spheres of consciousness that interlace, creating the noosphere of the human being:

### The plexus sphere of the human consciousness

The sphere of consciousness focused in the solar plexus region is associated with the creative aspect of the Goddess, with the principle of the so-called Red Goddess. The belly-focused consciousness enables the human being to be aware in each moment of what is going on around us as it relates to different dimensions of reality belonging either to the manifested or causal layers of life (described in the first part of our journey). This consciousness can move back and forth through different layers of Gaia's creation, coming instantly in contact with those aspects that we would like to perceive and those beings with whom we would like to communicate or collaborate.

### The back-related sphere of consciousness

The sphere of human consciousness related to the back space is associated with the principle of the Black Goddess, representing the path of change based upon the principle of wisdom. In this sense, the causal realms of consciousness at the back represent the resource of knowledge of how to face the winding paths of

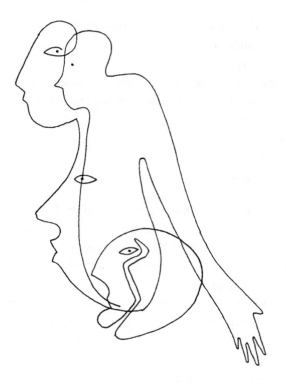

*The "three eyes of the Goddess" shows how consciousness*
*is distributed throughout the body*

personal development, and with it the accompanying challenges and transformations in relation to the collective destiny of humanity. Its sphere is focused at the back side of the body, below the loins.

### The head-focused consciousness

The eye of human consciousness focused in the head relates to the White Goddess aspect, standing for the quality of universal wholeness. It is usually called "the third eye." When active, it can hold us connected to all the different dimensions of the universe presented in the Intermezzo II in the form of the twelve-dimensional model of cosmic reality. Around its focus, at the center of the head, all dimensional extensions are held connected to human consciousness and can be approached in each moment to enter a given dimension.

## The second Chinese Wall

Now that we have gotten to know the consciousness sphere in its relationship to different parts of the body, my interest turns towards the cavity of the skull, presuming that it hides more secrets of consciousness yet to be decoded. But all my efforts to enter the dome of the head in a harmonious way ended in a senseless mental mess. Obviously there exists a severe blockade that does not allow the cavity of the head to be experienced in its true essence.

At the very beginning of our journey we came up against a similar blockade that I called "the second Berlin Wall," separating the manifested reality in front of the body from its causal complement behind the back. Now, almost at the end of our journey, at the point where the entrance to the space of the head seemed open, we come across another wall. It separates the sphere of the brain from the rest of the body. I call it "the second Chinese Wall."

The thousands of miles long Great Wall of China was built to prevent the "barbaric" tribes of the north from invading "the high culture" of the Chinese empire. In a similar way the second Chinese Wall is preventing the earthly quality of Gaia—considered of lower nature—to enter the "high temple" of the head.

I got to know the background to the second Chinese Wall blockade while trying to properly position focuses of Gaia and Sophia in my body. My search came about because I do not believe that both Sophia and Gaia would prefer to sit each in her own corner of the body, Gaia at its base and Sophia in the head. I find it more probable that the inspiration of Sophia passes through the whole body and finds its focus at its lower end. Accordingly, I searched upward for the focus of Gaia, in the direction of the head.

But when I arrived with my attention at the top of the throat, I was stopped by a massive wall, like the ones built in the Middle Ages to protect cities from enemies. The scene was as if in a film. High up on the wall I see a large group of demons with sticks in their hands, threatening and shouting that they do not allow this "woman with dirty shoes"—meaning Gaia—to enter "the sacred space of the head."

In my vision, the "second Chinese Wall" winds all around the brain, projecting the outdated pattern upheld by certain religious

### The Star of David exercise for focusing the cosmic and earthly inspirations within the body

1. Lift your angled arms over your head. Bring together the fingertips to make a triangle. By building the triangle you are about to focus the presence of Gaia at the crown of the head.

2. Lower your arms slowly, until they are diagonal, and stretch them out. When lowering them, imagine leading the cosmic inspiration of Sophia down toward the base of your body.

3. Bring your hands together there, keeping the elbows out to form a triangle directed downward to mark the focus of Sophia within your body.

4. Lifting the arms, straighten them slowly until they face diagonally upward. By lifting them, imagine leading the presence of Gaia upward through the body.

5. Then build again a triangle over your head to focus the presence of Gaia at its crown chakra.

6. Repeat the exercise a few times, and then observe silently what has been done inside of you.

dogmas and by some esoteric teachings, proclaiming the dominant role of "spiritual" dimensions in relation to the "earthly" realms. The higher dimensions are considered sacred, and the lower, Gaia-related ones are labeled profane.

To work on transmuting the blockade of the second Chinese Wall, I propose the Gaia Touch exercise called "the Star of David."

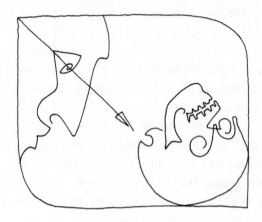

*Christ's skull exhibited in Paris*

According to the archetype of the Star of David, it directs the cosmic powers toward the core of the Earth, while the triangle with its peak turned upward opens the path of the earthly powers of Gaia upward toward the head.

### The doorway to the brain cavity

When starting to explore the body's inner organs, we first searched for the interdimensional portal that would enable us to enter the body's inner worlds. We found it behind the lower end of the breastbone. Does a similar portal exist to allow us to enter the brain cavity? In answer to the question, my intuition points toward the aperture at the bottom of the skull, where it touches the spine.

With this answer, I instantly remembered an impressive dream I had years ago that I never could properly understand:

*I am driving to Paris. It is extremely difficult to make progress on the French roads. Policemen have erected roadblocks to check travelers. Finally I learn that it is about transporting the precious skull of Christ to Paris to be exhibited in a grand international show.*

*In the next sequence I am looking at the skull of Christ at the exhibition. It is set inside a glass cube, and so placed that one can look through the spinal aperture in its base into the empty brain case. The hollow eye holes stare upward toward the ceiling of the exhibition hall.*

After awakening, I understood immediately that the skull of Jesus the Christ, put on display at the exhibition in such a humiliating position, represented, in the framework of the Western culture, the worst possible desecration. It also symbolized a dangerous reversal. Instead of paying attention to Christ's teaching, the empty skull was put on show.

Yet considering the position of the displayed skull, and seen in the context of the above-mentioned intuition, I suppose that the dream also had something to say in relation to my attempt to enter the brain cavity in a proper way. In my imagination I turned my skull slowly into the position suggested by the dream. To my surprise a beam of milky white light entered the space of my head from above via the spinal aperture. Without a trace of doubt, I associated its quality with the cosmic presence of Sophia, the feminine aspect of divinity.

The key to entering the inner space of the head had been found. But before we start to explore the different dimensions of the brain cavity, I would like to propose the following Gaia Touch exercise as a tool to working on opening the head to the cosmic dimension of consciousness by grounding it in the core of Gaia.

This exercise was revealed to me during my preparation for a workshop in 1999 on the island of Manhattan, New York. Being rooted deeply in the core of the Earth, the granite body of Manhattan can carry the extremely heavy city structure on its shoulders, and yet is capable of nourishing its highly creative cultural layers.

Through the exercise, the possibility is offered to us by the soul of Manhattan to ground our mental activity in the core of Gaia, while at the same time "our head" is opened to the whole spectrum of universal wisdom.

### The frozen treasure of the head

Now that the interdimensional door to the brain cavity has been found, what prevents us from entering its inner space? Is there a third blockade hiding the treasure of the head from us, even though we are its Gaia-appointed "managers"?

These general blockades of the human brain cavity were obviously installed to push us as human beings toward becoming

## MANHATTAN EXERCISE FOR THE GROUNDING OF THE HEAD

1. Bow forward, so that you almost touch the Earth with your hands stretched out. While doing so, imagine that with your hands you are reaching to the core of the Earth.

2. Get up slowly and, while doing this, imagine raising your connection with the core of the Earth upward along the vertical axis.

3. Bring your hands together in a downward prayer gesture. The fingertips are pointing downward, until you arrive at the height of your chest. At the level of your heart, they start pointing upward.

4. Lift up your hands further. When you have reached the height of your face, rest for a moment holding the prayer gesture in front of your third eye. Be aware that through this you have entered the inner space of the head through the interdimensional portal of the spinal aperture.

5. After a while, stretch out your arms horizontally to the left and to the right as wide as possible. Do it slowly! While making the gesture, imagine that in effect you are extending the field of your consciousness from within.

6. After that, bow toward the Earth again, and start the exercise from the beginning. Repeat a few times.

exclusively head-centered beings, living in a sophisticated mixture of high-tech civilization and esoteric spam. I believe it represents the challenge that we as a human race have called upon ourselves during the epoch of our blind search for absolute personal freedom. It can be understood as a challenge generated by the Mistress of Darkness. We have met this aspect of Sophia in the previous part of our journey.

Before turning attention to the newly surfacing third blockade, I will briefly summarize the two already discovered blockades of our brain cavity:

- The first blockade prevents the personal elemental being from access to the brain cavity in its rounds through the body. We learned of this through the dream of the Horse Trainers.

- The blockade of the second Chinese wall prevents the inspiration of Gaia from reaching the brain cavity and hinders the impulses of Sophia to reach down through the whole body. Its aim is to split the human being as a "spiritual being" away from our identity as beings of the Earth.

The third trauma of the human head was revealed to me in a dream that I received in the midst of the preparations to enter the brain cavity and to decode its secrets. The dream points toward the loss of skull's sacredness and urged me to search for its last traces:

*I have the feeling of standing in the sanctuary of a temple. My attention is directed toward a square niche in the wall at the side. (Its volume later makes me think of the brain cavity.) It feels as if I am looking into a large and sacred space. In effect, I can see traces of dark red stripes that once were framing the niche, underlying its sacred meaning. The niche itself is empty.*

Are there traces to be found of the sacred dimension of the head cavity, as indicated by the dream?

The traces of the red stripes from the dream can be associated with a geometric light structure I can see framing the space of the skull. I am amazed by the mathematical perfection of the light structure, vibrating in constant minute movements, enabling the brain cavity to be in connection with the noosphere of the Earth and the universe. It reminds me of the halo appearing in religious paintings around the heads of saints.

The halo framing the head finds its complement in a similar structure positioned around the whole body, which I described when observing the consciousness behind the human skeleton. In that case the light structure was around the focus of the perfect presence in the cavity of the belly, while it interacted with the minerals of the skeleton.

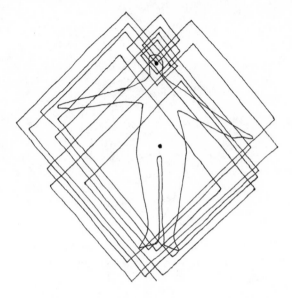

*The two crystal structures around the body and the head*

The geometric light structure framing the head does not interact with the body as the whole. It reveals the head as a separate holon of the body. The sphere of the head has a position in relation to the body similar to that of the Moon in relation to the Earth.

Similarly, as the Moon is responsible for the rhythmical movements within the water body of the Earth, my perception reveals that the central focus of the brain cavity is giving rhythm to the movements of the water element within the human body. The rhythm-generating focus of the brain is on one side attuned to the cosmic rhythms of Sophia, and on the other side I see the micro-crystals of the brain vibrating in resonance with the core of Gaia.

Similarly, as the focus in the belly moves the mineral structures of the body, the focus at the center of the brain represents the agents behind the movements of the liquid streams in the body. They complement each other with masculine/feminine polarity, mirroring the Earth/Moon relationship—as far as their cooperation is not disturbed by the aforementioned blockades.

In Venice, I was inspired by the Basilica of Saint Mark with the following Gaia Touch exercise to attune the pelvic and brain cavities to each other and restore the sacredness of the head.

GAIA TOUCH EXERCISE TO RE-ATTUNE THE BRAIN CAVITY
TO THE REGION OF THE HEART AND THE FOCUS OF THE
PERFECT PRESENCE IN THE BELLY

1. Sit down in silence for some moments. Relax by breathing in and out a few times.

2. Imagine that your head is a sphere of light.

3. Imagine that you grab this sphere with both hands and bring it down carefully to the level of your heart, positioning it into your heart space.

4. It is important to perform the corresponding gesture: starting with your hands positioned on both sides of your head, move them down parallel toward the chest, as if holding the head.

5. Keep the sphere of the head in the middle of the chest to attune it to your heart system.

6. Then imagine moving the sphere even one level lower, carrying it through your back space to position it within your pelvic cavity.

7. Let it rest there for a few moments to connect to your focus of the perfect presence.

8. Then imagine that it becomes as light as a soap bubble to be able to ascend vertically to its proper place, uniting again with your physical head.

9. Give thanks, and trust from now on your multidimensional intelligence.

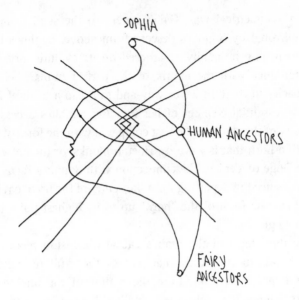

*The causal dimensions of the brain cavity*

## The causal dimension of the brain cavity

It should not be overlooked that the head space is also organized according to the binary principle. At the front side of the skull there is the face with chin, mouth, eyes, forehead, and ears. The back side is rounded and closed. The front is related to the manifested world, vibrating in front of the body. The back is related to the causal dimensions of the brain cavity.

There are three levels to the relationship of the causal dimension of the brain cavity:

• The first level is connected to the lowest positioned portion of the brain, emerging from the backbone, which the rational mind sees as the heritage of the animal brain. According to my perception, the brain bulge, at the top of the backbone, vibrates in resonance with the fairy world. It connects the human brain with the subtle consciousness body that we inherited from our fairy ancestors (as presented during the first part of our journey). Along this path the inspiration of the fairy world enters the brain cavity, enabling the human beings to think in harmony with Gaia's wisdom, will, and purpose.

- In a symmetrical way, Gaia's ascent to the skull from below is mirrored by Sophia's descent from above. Sophia's impulse is to inspire humanity to proceed on its evolutionary path in accordance with the matrix of the perfect human being. The capacity to think in a free way and to act in a truthful manner is an essential element of her impulse. Sophia's access to the cavity of the skull can be best compared with the form of the hat with a horn that is worn by Tibetan monks, or the hat worn by the Doge of Venice. The connection with Sophia's focus can be experienced if, departing from the center of the brain cavity, one follows the form of the "horn" up to its highest point (see the drawing).

- The third level of the brain's causal dimension relates to the back side of the skull. That part of the skull resonates with the impulses arriving from the realms of the ancestors and descendents. It enables the individual human being to trespass the limits of its own mind and to think in accordance with the logos of humanity as a whole.

With respect to the head's causal level, the center of the brain cavity is of key importance. This is the point of interconnection for all three impulses mentioned above. Through this interconnection, the core of the brain cavity comes into being—usually identified as the "third eye." The "third eye" does not exist at the forehead as often presented on esoteric paintings. Its proper place can be found if one follows with one's attention the paths of the three impulses, thus arriving to the place of their interaction.

The role of the core of the brain in the rhythm of the human water body has already been mentioned. Now we will take the step from the 7th to the 8th dimension of the "third eye"—referring to the model of the multidimensional space presented in the Intermezzo II—to discover its second role. In the 8th dimension, the "third eye" functions as a mirror, capable of turning the consciousness impulses of the earthly and universal noosphere outside-in, so that the brain can store them in its memory.

In this way a wonderful library comes into existence within our brain cavity, where the memory of interactions with the noosphere of the universe, the fairy worlds, the human race, and internal contemplation are stored. Indeed such a library of memory is desperately needed so that human beings can become autonomous thinkers, thinking in harmony with all other inhabitants of the Earthly Cosmos. In its halls it is possible to find instantly the proper knowledge that enables us as human beings to express our creative ideas, to formulate proper thoughts, and to speak the word.

## Gaia's creative hand and the human face

As mentioned, the human face represents that aspect of the skull that is open toward the manifested world. In accordance with its purpose, I see the model of Gaia's creative hand as the proper key to decode its essence:

The triangle at the palm of Gaia's creative hand can be associated with the three impulses vibrating at the causal level of the brain cavity—the impulses originating in the fairy world, the cosmos, and the world of ancestors and descendents. This relationship is identical to that of the matrix of the Earthly Cosmos, and finds its expression at the manifested level through the human face:

- The element of water expresses through the mouth and through our capability of creative speech (Gaia's forefinger).
- The element of fire expresses through the forehead and through our capability of mental concentration (Gaia's middle finger).
- The element of the earth manifests through the skin and through our capability to express through the power of the will (Gaia's ring finger).
- The element of air expresses through the nose and through our capability to move from one level of the universal noosphere to another (Gaia's little finger).
- The fifth element expresses through the eyes and ears, and through our capability to be present in the Earthly Cosmos as conscious, loving, and embodied beings (Gaia's thumb).

# 7

# THE MULTIDIMENSIONAL BODY

Traveling through the underground—the inner spaces—of the integral human body, we arrive at its deepest or densest layer. We are still within the material dimensions of the body, but we are looking at it from a different perspective. We have dived into the body's inner worlds, arriving at the inward side of manifested reality.

Seen from its causal side, how does the body that we know, that we wash and feed daily, look? The question is with respect to the material aspect of the body, which is usually familiar to the last detail. This view may be considered relative if the appearance of the body is perceived as only one of many possible expressions of Gaia consciousness.

*The human body and the five elements*

Before finishing our discussion of the relationship between the five elements and the human body, I need to make a clarification here. The classical concept that an individual soul requires mental, emotional, vital, and physical bodies in order for it to manifest in the physical world is not one I wish to deal with in this discussion.

There are two reasons to stay away from this concept:
- The concept emphasizes the impression that our body is separate from the essence of "the soul."
- The usual concept of the four bodies promotes the idea of the human being as a consumer of Gaia's products. As a consumer, the human race seems to give itself license to manipulate the four elements—which are the creative tools of Gaia—according to its own selfish needs.

Such a concept leaves humanity with no future. Instead of this concept, I would like to stress, while looking upon the creative hand of Gaia, the key importance of the fifth element and its interaction with the other four elements. Here is a short review of the five-element alternative to the stereotypical four-element body:

- The human water-element body is related to the phases of the Moon, as is the complete kingdom of the water element. The water body shows such a high grade of sensitivity that it enables the rosette of the individual soul to be present in the manifested world. Sensitivity to the phases of the Moon enables conversion of the rhythms of the cosmic cycles into the tissue of our plant-like organism.
- The light body, as an expression of the fire element consciousness, holds the heat of life force within our body so that we can exist as individual, mobile, and living beings. In this, our body is closely related to the animal kingdom.
- The earth-element body, which usually gets labeled "material," is a gift of the mineral kingdom, enabling us humans to exist as physically embodied beings working, loving, and moving within the framework of matter.
- The air-element body represents the personal noosphere, the individual sphere of consciousness. In effect the whole journey through the integral human body is based upon the vision that the body is primarily a specific constellation of consciousness aspects.
- The fifth-element body does not exist, as such. It enables the four bodies to cooperate in the sense of synergy. Representing the causal dimension of the four-element body, it connects in each successive moment the human presence on Earth to the matrix of the Earthly Cosmos.

The following Gaia Touch exercise emphasizes the relationship of the five-element body to the corresponding chakra system, described in the very beginning of our journey. In its context, the five elements can be experienced as part of our own being and not as something separate from us.

The relationship between the five elements and different parts of the body was explained in the Chapter 2 of the first part of our journey (see p. 29).

Here is the corresponding exercise:

GAIA TOUCH EXERCISE TO GET IN TOUCH WITH THE FIVE
ELEMENTS WITHIN THE BODY, WITH A DIAGRAM OF THE
FOUR-ELEMENT CHAKRA SYSTEM

1. We start by knocking three times at the center of the shoulders to mark the presence of the heart system, standing for
   the integrating fifth element. All five fingers are united into
   a fist while knocking upon the chest.

2. The exercise continues with the activation of the water element by rubbing for a while, with hands crossed, the two
   points on our chest below the clavicles. Here two chakras of
   the water element are located.

3. Afterward, we move to the element of fire. We rub the ear-
   lobes for a while, because two fire-element chakras are situated there. The hands do not cross this time.

4. Next is the element of earth. The corresponding chakras are
   located behind the knees. Tap with the hands crossed on your
   kneecaps.

5. And last we come to the element of air, with the chakras in
   the middle of the palms. To activate them, one should clap
   once in front of the body and once more behind the back.

6. Then start again by knocking upon the chest... Repeat the
   exercise at least three times.

## *The integral body — the body's future constitution*

The integral body dimension does not exist separately as some sort of alternative to our habitual body constitution. It also does not exist only in the future. It is already present within our body organism as potentialities to be awakened the moment human beings begin to understand that the present body constitution is over-manipulated and not capable of responding to the challenges of the planetary transmutation. Also important is awareness that the cosmic moment has arrived to move toward the integral body constitution. One by one, members of the human race are embodying the integral body dimension, an aspect of loving and integrating consciousness.

In effect, all the different dimensions of the human body and their relationship to the parallel evolutions that we have observed during our journey represent single units of the (future) integral body. They exist and function relatively separately in the "old" four-dimensional body. Some of them are reduced to their minimum influence, and many of them are totally suppressed. Yet they still exist as a potential that can be awakened, purified, and reconnected with all other elements to compose the "future" body.

The "past" body and the "future" body may show no difference at a glance. And yet there is a fundamental change required to make the transition from one to the other. During this transition —in effect, a body transformation—its whole inner constitution changes. But to be able to change in such a radical way, our body needs to be recognized and perceived inevitably as a specific form of consciousness. Then the organs do not need physically to move around in the body and our bodily forms do not need to change.

What happens can be imagined as a specific elevation in frequency. Due to this elevation, synergies become possible between the single units of our integral body, described during our tripartite journey through the extensions of the human body, which is understood as a microcosm of Gaia's Earth. One can sense a large number of possibilities opening for our future evolution. But better than to imagine, is to experience the new body constitution!

The following Gaia Touch hand cosmogram is designed to allow you to experience the transition from the traditional composition

### GAIA TOUCH HAND COSMOGRAM TO EXPERIENCE THE NEW BODY OF THE EARTHLY COSMOS

1. To represent the old body structure, the hands should form a sphere in such a way that the tips of the corresponding fingers, including the thumbs, touch each other. We have formed a closed sphere that has a one-dimensional character like the ball of the Earth seen as a material object spinning around the Sun.

2. To proceed toward the new body structure, which is multidimensional, we need to rotate one hand clockwise and the other counter-clockwise simultaneously (the finger tips touching), till we arrive at the following finger composition.

3. Both small fingers touch the tips of the thumbs. The other three fingers are directed toward the open space at the left and right. Instead of a closed ball of the body we have an open multidimensional structure allowing the breath of the Earth and the Universe to glide through.

4. The connection between both thumbs and the small fingers is important. It stands for the new driving force behind the human evolution and the evolution of the Earthly Cosmos. The connection represents the power of consciousness (the small fingers) coupled with the inspiration of our sister evolutions that we share with the beauty of the Earth (the thumbs in the role of the causal world).

of a four-element body being, toward the new body constitution—related to the human body as well as to the Earth as a planetary whole. It is based upon the previously presented resonance of the four elements on our hand. In this case the thumb stands for the integrating fifth element.

# CONCLUSION

The point has arrived where our journey through the extensions of the human body comes to an end. This does not mean that the exploration of the universe of the human body is concluded. Not at all! We witness only an attempt to bring awareness of the precious gift of embodying—a unique gift of Gaia. To bring awareness does not mean having the ambition to exhaust the theme to the last detail. The purpose of our journey through the three extensions of the integral human being, rather, is to point toward all the different dimensions and aspects of human existence within the Earthly Cosmos that are, to a large extent, ignored by modern civilization, or even suppressed.

I have tried to find the proper mode of expression for diverse phenomena that often unexpectedly appeared in front of my surprised eyes. My reactions are primarily the answers of an artist creating an art work. Often I was challenged with totally forgotten aspects of the body that demanded attention, sometimes even when a corresponding language to express their message did not exist and had to be invented anew.

My initial idea was to create a book that can be further developed by the reader. The basic text provides a background concerning different themes. But then there are Gaia Touch exercises along the path that offer the relevant possibility to continue the exploration in one's own way and to earn one's own experiences. This might be a proper way to bring about a silent revolution through which the rather humiliating human relationship to Gaia and her gift of embodiment in the Earthly Cosmos can be changed radically.

I wish to conclude with the Gaia Touch exercise of spinning an invisible thread, by which it is possible to manifest peace within oneself and one's environment. It was shown to me by a group of dwarfs on the island of Male Srakane in the Adriatic Sea. Its revelation started with a dream in which I saw how a furious man was silenced by a group of dwarfs with the help of a thin silvery

### SPINNING THE THREAD OF PEACE

1. Hold your hands in front of your chest, one hand above the other. Thumbs and ring fingers of each hand are touching each other.
2. Move both hands respectively upward and downward in rhythmical movement. The upper hand is moving downward and the lower upward.
3. The movement is only possible if the two fingers are opening up in the moment when the hands are about to meet each other.
4. Keep on with the movement for a while, and then dive into the silence that has built up.
5. Since the ring finger is the focus, this is a variation of the exercise in which the earth element is involved. To experience the peace offered by the other four elements, use another of the four fingers to touch the thumb. The principle of Gaia's creative hand, mirrored in the human hand, is the key.

thread wrapped around his body. Since I knew the point of communication with the dwarf community of that island, I went there asking them how to spin such a peace-creating thread. We may need such knowledge to be able to keep peace in the times of the expected deep changes within our body and around ourselves.

# LIST OF GAIA TOUCH EXERCISES

Crete exercise to strengthen the relationship with Gaia 11

Foot exercise to distinguish the qualities of the front and
the back spaces 17

Hand cosmogram to dissolve the wall separating the front
from the back sides of the body 19

To rinse particles of fear out of the body 22

To give thanks to the planetary network
of mountains and oceans 23

To experience the personal elemental being 33

To perceive the essence of plants 36

To experience the plant core of the body 37

To renew our plant-like body 41

Group exercise dedicated to our relationship with the animal world 47

Group ritual to relate to the fairy world 54

To connect with the personal elemental being and
the elemental self 57

To connect with the world of ancestors and descendents 65

To identify with your individual soul matrix 69

Meditation to experience our relationship as human beings
with the divine parents of the Earthly Cosmos 71

Bogomil Gesture to experience divinity at the center of your being 72

To transform the alienated personality 75

Personal ritual to support the liberation of the manifested world
from suppressing the human projections 82

Group ritual to honor all beings and worlds of the Earthly Cosmos 84

To embody new proportions between different aspects of
the human being 88

The threefold blessing of Gaia 100

To experience Gaia's creative process within oneself 105

To activate the personal water body 109

To embody the new role of the feminine and the masculine
principles within us 114

To lead the dragon powers to their original essence 119

To come in touch with the dragon powers within 125

Basel exercise for transforming the primeval powers into creative impulses 127

Ritual to connect to Gaia, the Mother of Life, and to Sophia, the Wisdom of the Universe 132

Gaia Touch exercise of protection with a double mandorla 134

The Healing Tear of Grace 136

Peace meditation with the Sword of Truth 139

Corcovado exercise to reconnect with the divinity within 143

To experience the angelic presence 148

To cooperate with the lithospheric angels in the transmutation processes 151

Gaia Touch exercise for activating human creative potentials 152

Gaia Touch key to glide through an interdimensional portal 158

To recreate the capacity of thinking in the integral way 171

To strengthen the link with the focus of the perfect presence 173

To reconnect with the personal elemental master 177

Hand cosmogram for grounding and for anchoring in the cosmic whole 183

Gaia Touch exercise of transmutation 192

Venetian Gaia Touch exercise to hold safe the thread of life 195

Peace meditation with the dove, the olive branch, and the muse of peace 200

To stimulate the re-creation of the embodied world structure 203

To experience the authentic quality of the heart system 205

To ground the heart center in the pelvic cavity 209

Humpolec exercise for balancing the matter of the Earth and the light of the universe 218

The Star of David exercise for focusing the cosmic and the earthly inspirations in the body 224

Manhattan exercise for the grounding of the head 227

To re-attune the brain cavity to the region of the heart and the focus of the perfect presence in the belly 230

To get in touch with the five elements within the body 236

Hand cosmogram to experience the new body of the Earthly Cosmos 238

Spinning the thread of peace 240

# LIST OF DRAWINGS

Crete exercise to strengthen the relationship with Gaia    11

The threefold path    13

Foot exercise to distinguish the qualities of the front
and the back spaces    17

Hand cosmogram to dissolve the wall separating the front
from the back sides of the body    19

Gaia Touch exercise to rinse particles of fear out of the body    22

Gaia Touch exercise to give thanks to the planetary network of
mountains and oceans    23

Gaia's creative hand    28

Beings of the Earth Element (dwarves) work on transforming
archetypes into vital forms    31

Gaia Touch exercise to experience the personal elemental being    33

Gaia Touch exercise to perceive the essence of plants    36

Gaia Touch exercise to experience the plant core of the body    37

The flute of Gaia    39

The manifested world and the 'liquid' world of the causal
dimension    43

Group exercise dedicated to our relationship with the
animal world    47

Animal resonance points upon the human body    49

Group ritual to relate to the fairy world    54

Gaia Touch exercise to connect with the personal elemental
being and the elemental self    57

How to imagine the elements of the fairy body as distributed
throughout the human organism    61

The three layers of the manifested world in relationship to
the causal dimensions — all in relationship to the human being    63

Gaia Touch exercise to connect with the world of ancestors
and descendents    65

Gaia Touch exercise to identify with your individual soul matrix    69

Bogomil gesture to experience divinity at the center of your being    72

Gaia Touch exercise to transform the alienated personality    75

Personal ritual to support the liberation of the manifested
world from the suppressing human projections    82

Group ritual to honor all beings and worlds of the
Earthly Cosmos      84

Gaia Touch exercise to embody new proportions between
different aspects of the human being      88

The horizontal axis of life and the vertical axis of creation      89

Gaia's creative hand at the consciousness level      91

The fish woman Faronika from a medieval fresco in Slovenia      97

The threefold blessing of Gaia      100

Gaia Touch exercise to experience Gaia's creative process
within oneself      105

The Atlantic and Pacific oceans related to the human body      107

Gaia Touch exercise to activatre the personal water body      109

Pan as the Celtic god Cernunos, perceived in a park in
Turnich, Germany      111

Author's cosmogram dedicated to the balance between
the feminine and the masculine principles      113

Gaia Touch exercise to honor the new role of the
feminine and masculine principles within us      114

The place of dragons in the relationship between Gaia and
the human being      116

Gaia Touch exercise to lead the dragon powers to their
original essence      119

The three dragons on a painted stone from Gotland      121

The genealogy of dragons up to the point when the primary
forces of Gaia become embodied in matter      122

The creative bridge of the primeval powers      124

Exercise to come in touch with the dragon power within      125

Basel exercise for transforming the primeval powers into
creative impulses      127

The human being in relation to the extensions of the
Earthly Cosmos      129

Ritual to connect to Gaia, the Mother of Life, and to Sophia,
the Wisdom ot the Universe      132

Two mandorla forms in the urban structure of Venice with
their focal points      133

Gaia Touch exercise of protection with a double mandorla      134

The Healing Tear of Grace      136

Peace meditation with the Sword of Truth      139

Sophia, Gaia, and Christ in the vision of Hildegard von Bingen 142
Corcovado exercise to reconnect with the divinity within 143
My vision of the angelic presence in the three basilicas
of Andrea Palladio in Venice 147
Gaia Touch exercise to cooperate with the lithospheric angels
in the transmutation processes 151
Gaia Touch exercise for activating human creative potentials 152
The sand clock form and zero point of an interdimensional
portal 157
Gaia Touch key to glide through an interdimensional portal 158
A spherical model of the 12-dimensional blueprint 161
The personal elemental being interacting with the human
individuality 167
The dream with the horse trainers 169
Gaia Touch exercise to recreate the capacity of thinking
in the integral way 171
Gaia Touch exercise to strengthen the link with the focus
of the perfect presence 173
The image from the dream with the personal elemental master 175
Gaia Touch exercise to reconnect with the personal elemental
master 177
The dream of the alienated city 177
Hand cosmogram for grounding and for anchoring
in the cosmic whole 183
The dream about the black skin layer 186
The water body held in place through the fire element
structure 189
Gaia Touch exercise of transmutation 192
Venetian Gaia Touch exercise to hold safe the thread of life 195
Hildegard von Bingen's vision of the integral human being 197
Peace meditation with the dove, the olive branch, and the
muse of peace 200
Gaia Touch exercise to stimulate the re-creation of the
embodied world structure 203
Santiago di Compostela gesture of opening the heart 205
The constellation of the heart centers 207
Gaia Touch exercise to ground the heart system in the
pelvic cavity 209

The heart space comes into being throughthe interaction
between the powers of the pelvic cavity and the lemniscate
of the heart centers                                                            213

The double vortex of body organs                                                216

Humpolec exercise for balancing the matter of the Earth
and the light of the universe                                                   218

The "three eyes of the Goddess" show how consciousness
is distributed throughout the body                                              222

The Star of David exercise for focusing the cosmic and
the earthly inspirations within the body                                        224

Christ's skull exhibited in Paris                                               225

Manhattan exercise for grounding of the head                                    227

The two crystal structures around the body and the head                         229

Gaia Touch exercise to re-attune the brain cavity to the region
of the heart and the focus of the perfect presence in the belly                 230

The causal dimensions of the brain cavity                                       231

Gaia Touch exercise to get in touch with the five elements
within the body, with a diagram of the four-element
chakra system                                                                   236

Gaia Touch hand cosmogram to experience the new body
of the Earthly Cosmos                                                           238

Spinning the thread of peace                                                    240